Bird Gardening

Brian Loomes

DALESMAN

First Published in Great Britain 1993 by
Dalesman Publishing Company Limited,
Stable Courtyard, Broughton Hall,
Skipton, North Yorkshire BD23 3AE
Text © 1993 Brian Loomes

ISBN **1 85568 060 2**
Typeset by **Lands Services, East Molesey, Surrey.**
Printed by **Biddles Ltd, Guildford, Surrey.**

Contents

Introduction

THIS BOOK IS for those who would like to attract wild birds to visit and perhaps nest in their gardens. You can do this whether you have a tiny backyard in a city centre, a suburban semi-detached garden, or a country estate of many acres. The pleasure of bird life is available to all.

I am not an expert either on birds or gardens, as any expert will confirm. But I am experienced in making my own garden work for me as both a garden and a sort of small bird sanctuary at the same time. If I can do it in my own inexpert way, then so can you. The chapters that follow will suggest ways of going about this based on how I did it myself.

This book will not describe birds in recognition terms. That is the job of a specialist bird book, which you will probably need to help identify the birds that visit you. The notes on individual birds here are set out purely in terms of what steps may be taken to cater for their particular needs and tastes.

I am no photographer either, but I did take many of the photographs in this book myself with the aid of a very mediocre old camera. The better photographs were taken by a friend, Paul Reinsch, with better equipment and more patience. The photographs were all taken in my own garden in one season, 1990. They may not win any prizes but they do show birds that have been attracted to feed and nest along with the nestboxes and feeders they came to use.

The whole point of the book is that it is written and illustrated by an amateur for amateurs. If I can do it, then surely you can do it as well or better. Good luck, and enjoy your bird gardening.

Brian Loomes

1
Garden, Sanctuary or Both?

THE PURPOSE OF this book is to help owners of gardens, however small, to attract wild birds to visit and, hopefully, to nest. How do we modify an existing garden, or even construct one from scratch, with this particular aim in mind? Much will depend on how far the individual owner wishes to go, and to what expense.

Gardens are areas of constant change. New owners want to alter an existing garden. Long-resident owners often feel like adding a new feature or altering an old one. Let us look at the garden from the point of view of, assuming some construction or change is to take place anyway, which features may be added or removed which will help in attracting birds.

The first question that needs to be asked is: what is your garden for? What do you expect from it? Is it there so that you can enjoy plants or flowers, a lawn, or a sun-bathing area? And where amongst the scheme of things does the attraction of birds fall for you personally? Is it high in your priorities or very much secondary? In Britain the weather prevents most of us from being out in the garden for more than half the year, except in the case of the dedicated, who will work outside regardless of the weather. On the other hand, we can enjoy bird life in our gardens through the window at any time and in any weather. A bird table sited within view of the kitchen window will be a source of interest and pleasure every day of the year. If we hope to have something more interesting than starlings and house sparrows to watch, we have to take some steps towards encouraging a bigger variety of birds.

Fifteen years ago the 'garden' which came with my house was simply a fenced-off piece of meadowland and bog. It was large, far too large for any real garden, amounting to three acres in all. It was fortunately sited in the countryside in the Yorkshire Dales, so there was ample bird life within distance. But precious few birds nest in open meadow and I doubt if there were more than two or three pairs of nesting birds in the whole three acres. Today there are scores of pairs of birds of many kinds and we have probably in excess of 50 pairs of birds who nest and rear their young with us each season. I long ago stopped counting and am content simply to enjoy them.

Each person will interpret bird gardening in his own way and to suit his personal concept of the kind of garden he wants, based, of course, on its size first of all. Many will want a 'pretty' bit with lawns and flower beds as the most visible features, and might think in terms of their bird gardening efforts as being mainly at the end furthest away from the house. There is some sense in this, as birds at the far end of the garden suffer less disturbance from people and pets such as cats. The bird table, however, will probably be required close to the house, otherwise feeding birds will go mostly unobserved and filling the bird table becomes a chore, especially in bad weather.

What, then, are we trying to create? What requirements do birds have that they might find more readily in nature than in our artificial gardens and how can we redress the imbalance? Obvious things are food and water, which are dealt with later. Obvious, too, is a place to nest. But what else? Are we hoping to create a natural jungle, a wood, a forest, a wilderness where nature is left to run riot? Not at all. Neglected areas become choked with weeds and brambles. Trees and shrubs there become attenuated or smothered. In fact, dense thickets and woods contain few birds, certainly few nesting birds.

Garden birds come to gardens for a reason, and that reason is because some gardens contain the conditions they seek. Of these, the first essential is safety. Ideal conditions for most garden birds consist of open areas interspersed with bushes and trees. From the bushes they can see the safety of open areas and from the open areas they can escape, if need be, to the concealment of shrubs. You have only to witness a predator such as a kestrel chasing a small bird such as a blue tit to observe that the only chance it has of escaping is to dodge through the shrubbery where the kestrel cannot follow nimbly enough. In the open such a bird is doomed by the kestrel's greater speed.

Many gardens happen by sheer chance to combine these two factors – an open area of lawn or vegetable plot or yard at the centre with herbage, shrubs and trees round the edges. Only certain birds enjoy lawns for their own sakes – principally worm-eaters such as thrushes and blackbirds. But all birds enjoy the open field of view provided by a lawn, which gives a clear view of approaching danger. So, by happy chance, many gardens already have this sort of basic layout. Our aim is to improve it to the maximum, whilst still keeping the garden plan to suit the owner's personal taste.

Where to start? Your garden will probably have some sort of enclosure – a wall, a fence or a hedge. Many hedgerows are disappearing today through modern agricultural practices. As youngsters we used to search field hedges for birds' nests. Today you would have trouble finding any field hedges to search. Lots of hedge-nesting birds are looking for a new home, so a hedge will be a big attraction to many species. In fact, most of the commoner garden birds will nest or shelter in hedges.

What sort of hedge? Hawthorn is my favourite. If grown from rooted cuttings, such as you can buy reasonably at a garden centre, it is going to take the best part of ten years to get a decent hedge thick enough for birds to nest in. Young hawthorn hedgings need pruning each year (for our purpose, that is) even if only by a minute amount. This makes them throw out more sideshoots and grow more densely, whilst keeping some sort of shape to the hedge itself. Pruning also encourages the leaf cover to grow; that is, the top 'layer' of leaves, which makes for concealment for nests and birds. Don't prune your hedge, and you'll end up with a row of sticks with leaves on top.

Beech also makes a fine hedge and may come to chest height a little quicker than hawthorn. Again beech hedgings must be pruned as they grow, to force shoots to spring out from low down. Otherwise they will grow thin and lank and your hedge will have more parts open than filled. Once at the required height, you will need to trim the hedge each year, and in the case of a beech hedge, this causes dead leaves to remain in place through the winter, giving some winter as well as summer, cover, and therefore forming an attraction for early nesters.

Both hawthorn and beech hedges provide nest sites for such birds as thrushes, blackbirds, hedge sparrows and most of the finches. Both types have their attractions and if you have a hedge along more than one side of your garden, there's no reason you could not have one side of hawthorn and the other of beech.

Cupressus (lawsoniana or other) makes a marvellous hedge and is quicker growing than hawthorn or beech, giving a nesting hedge within five years. Some people take against it as being a foreigner but birds neither know that nor care, and it probably provides more nesting sites than any other species. Being evergreen, it gives cover all year round, and privacy, if that is a feature you look for in your garden. Again, a small amount of pruning is desirable year by year. Once the desired height is reached, you can trim it annually like any other hedge.

Uniformity is not sought by birds: quite the contrary. If you have three different hedges along three sides of your garden, birds might well prefer that to one species all round. Hedges often benefit from an occasional tree standing proud from them. You are going to need some sort of larger trees in your bird garden, if only as roosting and singing posts. Some suggested species are set out below, but you have the choice (with a new hedge) of setting the occasional tree in the hedge itself, taking care not to cut it back when trimming the rest. You can do this quite nicely in a hedge of beech or hawthorn, but less so for cupressus, where the denser growth may stifle it. My suggestions for trees to set in a hedge would be mountain ash and birch, for reasons explained later. Much depends on your space.

If your garden has a fence, maybe of the larchlap or interwoven panel type, then a hedge planted inside that will make a doubly attractive nesting place, the fence giving greater protection and cover from the outside.

Many gardens will already have some established trees, maybe quite mature and tall ones, and if so, well and good. In this case, you already have a nucleus for birds in the insect life of a mature tree as well as a site to fix nest boxes. If not, you will certainly want some specimen trees unless your site is very small.

If planting a new hedge, you could choose to plant your trees in the hedge itself, but trees planted a yard or two inside the garden from the hedge are preferable if space allows, as each tree is then usable along its full trunk for positioning a nest box at whatever height is needed.

Those who have a lot of space, a lot of patience, and like acorns, can plant oak trees. They are very slow-growing and provide few nest sites except when very ancient. Fine trees, yes, but if your number of large trees must be limited because of space, then forget oak.

Ash, elm, alder and sycamore provide few nest sites till very old and even then usually only through fissures and cracks, which we can simulate better and many years sooner. Of these, the latter two grow fastest. Sycamore leaves and shoots give off a sticky goo, which attracts wasps and puts me off them. If you have patience, you can prune sycamores once they reach about ten feet in such a way as to force them to produce multi-fork branches, which might just make nest sites for thrushes, blackbirds or chaffinches, but generally the leaf cover is a bit thin for this. I've tried it, but nothing ever nested in my forks. Willows of whatever kind can be pruned in the same way and these will throw many shoots from the pruning point, but again I've had nothing nest in mine.

Beech are slow-growing initially but soon take off and make fine specimen trees. However, after a very few years they give off a toxic drip with the result that nothing else will grow under a beech. They produce few nest sites, except when clipped and restrained to the size of a tall bush. Clipped beech, even quite tall ones, will retain their leaves in winter and produce multi-forked branches which, with the leaf cover, will offer good nest sites for thrushes and many other small birds such as greenfinches and linnets.

All the above trees will grow very tall and have little value for birds except as providers of insects and as singing or perching posts – but all trees provide the latter anyway. Ask yourself, do you really want tall trees which are slow-growing? Will they take all the sunlight from your garden? Have you room for trees in excess of 50 feet tall with a spread of 30 feet or more? If you have a large plot and you like these trees, then fine, but they offer little for bird gardeners.

So what about some trees that don't take up too much space and have additional benefits? Mountain ash are wonderful trees. They stay in a restrained shape and size, seldom exceed twenty feet fully grown, and are covered in flowers and then red berries that many birds will eat in autumn. They look well, provide beauty and food, and don't mind pruning if you like to keep things to a certain shape or area. They seldom provide nest sites, but you can't have everything.

Birch, sometimes called silver birch, are neat little trees, grow anywhere easily, look well, and provide good feeding for numerous small birds. Ours are constantly full of titmice. They don't usually grow above 25 feet high and in immature form may have dense branches which can provide nest sites for such birds as finches.

For nest sites, especially early in the season, you cannot beat Cypress such as Cupressus lawsoniana or any of the similar varieties sold in every nursery, some of them of interesting colours. Once you get them started, they will grow rapidly and by the time they reach six feet high, thrushes and blackbirds and perhaps finches and woodpigeons will be desperate to nest in them. If they get too tall, then lop off the tops with a saw. I've regularly trimmed the top six feet of some of mine and they seem no worse for it, though obviously you lose the conical shape. They will stand pruning or trimming as much as you like and whenever you like (true gardeners please forgive me!) and will grow the denser for it. Cupressus are my kind of tree. I've no time for delicate, temperamental trees that die if you show them a pair of secateurs. With Cupressus you can do whatever you want, even trimming off all the lower branches up to six foot to leave a bare trunk for a nestbox position.

Larch are beautiful conifers, which lose their leaves in winter, when they look really dead, but grow dense and handsome in summer.

They provide nest sites and food for many birds and will intermix well in small clumps with Cupressus, or they will stand proud as single specimens, when they will spread out wide. If they get too tall, you can lop off the tops and they'll survive.

You can buy tiny two- or three-year-old spruce from a nursery for a few pence each, if you have the patience to wait half a dozen years for them to reach a useful size. Or you can buy them anywhere from three to six feet tall rooted in pots so that they will plant easily, as indeed you can with Cupressus and larch. Buying trees above six feet high means considerable expense and difficulty in planting them. What you are buying with taller trees is time, and it is up to you whether you want an instant garden or can wait. If you want some starter trees of a decent size then Cupressus are probably the most useful as a foundation, with larch and spruce in smaller sizes. I would not suggest buying anything over six feet high, as they will more easily blow over and will need strong stakes for some years.

Spruce trees exist in various forms (Sitka spruce, Norway spruce, etc.) but to you and me they are all Christmas trees. Spruce grow rapidly – roughly a foot a year for the first half-dozen years, then three feet a year thereafter. Larch and Cupressus grow at about the same rapid rate. Spruce are dense and make good nesting sites, especially early in the season as, of course, they are evergreens.

The principle of an ideal bird 'garden', as we said earlier, is one of dense patches of cover with open spaces around. If you have space, plant Cupressus in clusters of three or four together, maybe four feet apart. Their branches will then grow into each other and make a tiny dense jungle of foliage offering more nest sites sooner than single trees might. They are also more wind-resistant that way. A single spruce tree can be a spidery thing at times and spruce have that annoying habit of growing nicely for a number of years, then suddenly dying on you for no apparent reason, or even dying back on just some of the branches. This can come as a bit of a blow if it is ten years in to your growing plan. Planting in clusters helps avoid this, as they won't *all* suddenly die on you.

Scots pine are pretty trees but little use for nesting in their first twenty years except for the occasional chaffinch in a fork, which would just as soon nest in something else. I like to see one or two Scots pine about anyway, but they have little to offer as nest sites.

Holly can offer nesting cover and today various fancy forms can be bought, some of which provide heavy crops of berries, useful for Christmas decoration if the birds don't eat them all first. We have one mature holly which produces lots of berries by November but has been stripped by birds before Christmas, when we have to go out and buy some. There are even thornless hollies today – we bought one once and rabbits ate it within a week, so now we know why hollies have prickles. Most hollies are very slow-growing and need patience if bought tiny. If you want berries, don't buy a male tree as males don't bear fruit. They will grow a denser cover if you prune them, and will offer nest sites for blackbirds and thrushes. Personally I find them too slow-growing, and whatever they offer for nesting is provided more quickly by Cupressus or spruce.

Laurel is sometimes recommended for nest sites. It is very slow-growing and I always think it a bit of a gloomy plant reminiscent of dark Victorian shrubberies. I planted half a dozen some fifteen years ago, which have just reached six feet in height and have yet to hold their first nest. Additionally, the leaves exude a sweet juice in spring, which attracts wasps like a magnet, so I cannot recommend them. Here in the country we always have two or three wasps' nests in the garden each season, and on two separate occasions wasps have taken over unused tit boxes and once a swarm of bees moved into another one. So we see more than our share of wasps without planting anything to attract more. Whilst on the subject of wasps, it is worth mentioning that cotoneasters are sometimes recommended for bird gardens because of the red fruits, which birds love. Wasps love them too, so be warned if thinking of planting one by your doorway.

Elders are liked by birds for their berries. They will grow quickly into small trees if left but can be kept clipped to bush size, when they will make a more dense leaf cover and produce possible nest sites for blackbirds, thrushes and finches. One thing they don't always tell you about elders is that vicious midges breed on their leaves in great numbers, so if you propose planting elders, you want them as far from the house as possible. Have one if you must, but you have been warned. An occasional elder in a hedge helps with leaf cover.

Fruit trees can be a nice addition to any garden – apples, pears, plums, cherries. We have a few, which the birds certainly enjoy. The trouble is they seldom leave any for us. Windfalls left on the ground will help feed birds and hedgehogs in winter.

Yew and box are fine if you have established examples in your garden. They are slow-growing, however, and those that plant them may not live long enough to see the results come of age.

A friend of mine was once throwing out a number of ancient rose trees and bush roses. Rather than see them destroyed, we stuck them in a distant part of a hedge as fillers, where they were left to grow wild. Every year they are covered in dozens of rose-hips, which birds dearly enjoy.

Brambles will creep across the ground and root themselves here and there if allowed to, when they are nothing but a nuisance. Instead, it is possible to build a small framework by sticking three or four tree stakes or fence posts into the ground and train the brambles around them, helped by a few wire strands. As many as half a dozen different varieties can be grown round this, like runner beans around a wigwam of pea sticks. This provides fruit for people and birds and, after a year or two of leaving dead stalks in place, a nesting site for finches or blackbirds or thrushes. Wild or cultivated blackberries can be trained round any old tree stump or fallen branch. Grasses will grow up into the tangle and make a nesting site for hedge sparrows or robins. Wild or cultivated forms of honeysuckle can be trained in the same way.

Hawthorn can be grown as a single specimen tree, as well as in hedge form. With pruning and trimming, a neat shape can be achieved and pruning also makes for closer leaf-cover growth. Hawthorns can provide good nesting cover and, if not pruned too often, berries in autumn, as well as showing handsome flowers early in the year. They can be well into leaf by late April, encouraging early nesters. Once a hawthorn gets to tree size, say about twelve feet high, it often thins our considerably (though judicious pruning earlier in its life may help avoid this) and it then becomes difficult to prune at that height. As a tree hawthorn provides increasingly fewer nesting sites the taller it gets – ultimately only for such birds as woodpigeons and magpies in the upper twigs of chaffinches in the forks. Kept as a hedge or as a tall single bush, hawthorn offers far more nesting possibilities.

Apart from the boundary hedge (or fence-with-hedge) and the boundary specimen trees, it is an idea to have a few specimen trees here and there throughout the garden. Remember when planting that some trees do develop a very wide branch spread and the plan is not to fill the plot like a wood, which is counter-productive. Birds avoid coming down to a lawn if it is too hemmed in by tall hedges or trees. They like a good open and well-lit area around, so that cats and other predators cannot creep up on them unobserved.

If your garden is big enough, your boundary 'hedge' can become a boundary 'wood' by growing random trees and shrubs for a few feet, even a few yards, from the hedge itself – a sort of ribbon of woodland all round your garden. The principle of open spaces with protective blocks of cover applies at all times, so you may need to tailor your actions according to what trees are in adjoining gardens and how dense they are.

Ivy is a marvellous evergreen plant, which needs no attention apart from trimming if it gets too high. Clippings can themselves often be planted to make more plants, as they have many roots along the stems. You can buy a rooted plant from a nursery to start off or pull a few stems from a friend's garden. It is pointless to try to plant a piece more than about a foot long, as, if it takes, it tends to die back to the last foot anyway, and dying back (or dying totally) tends to be more common with longer stems. There are all manner of variegated ivies today, but they are all the same to a bird looking for a nest site. Quantity is better than quality for their purpose. Big-leaf varieties suit birds better than small, giving greater screen cover. Two or three stems against a house wall or outbuilding, or even a fence will produce an abundance of nest sites in a few years. We have had pied wagtails, blackbirds, thrushes, chiffchaffs, wrens, spotted flycatchers and chaffinches all nesting in ivy on what were formerly just two bare walls when we bought the house. Ivy seems to thrive quite well without any fuss just by sticking the roots into the ground, even building-site clay beside a new house wall. It will take three years or more before it is big enough for nesting cover. Increased spread can be gained by planting two or three stems a few feet apart.

Virginia creeper is deciduous and grows well against house walls too, often with spectacular effect, particularly in autumn when the leaves turn red. This is not in full leaf till well into May and perhaps on that account our own birds seem to prefer to nest in ivy on the very same wall and ignore the Virginia creeper. Some house owners fear that ivy or other wall climbers will destroy masonry by rooting into the mortar. Some, however, argue that rain runs off the leaves and down the stems rather than down the house wall, so to some degree this helps keep the house walls dry. Both ivy and Virginia creeper are self-climbing and need no support after the first year or so.

Ivy will often grow well up the trunks of old trees or even remaining stumps of trees, where it can make excellent nest sites. Some claim if it gets too old and thick and surrounds a tree, it may strangle the tree. If it seems in danger of reaching that stage, cut it back a bit to give the tree a fresh chance. Don't let ivy or any other climber get under the roof slates, as it will work its way unseen into the loft and causes the slates to lift. It is better to cut it back four or five feet below the eaves once a year – less than that and you'll have to do it two or three times a year. Ivy grown on a boundary wall makes a popular nest site.

Some clematis plants will also make very fine wall cover and grow bushy and thick with a covering of wonderful flowers. Hedge sparrows, blackbirds, thrushes and pied wagtails nest regularly in ours, which in parts is so dense that we cannot see the nests, even though we see the birds flying in and out to feed young. Again, keep it out of the roof slates. Clematis has to be tied to the wall. Grow types such as Montana, which does not have to be cut back each season, as you want a good year-by-year build up of density.

Climbing roses will grow as high as the roof eaves if allowed to and provide decoration along with nest sites. They come into leaf early so provide much-needed cover to the first nesters of the season. All climbers love south-facing walls, and so do birds nesting in them. One climbing rose we have has passed bedroom window height and holds a nest each year, usually a chaffinch but this year a high-rise song thrush at fourteen feet. It is a particular thrill to be able to look out of the window right into a nest.

Often at the 'bottom of the garden' there are areas of neglect – old vegetable plots you always meant to do something about but which now stand chest-high in nettles or thistles. Such clusters of weeds can themselves be attractive hunting grounds for birds. By all means confine your weeds to certain patches, but eradicating them may be a mistake. Many finches, including goldfinches, love thistle heads, and you can buy certain monster thistles, which will help attract them and look pretty too. Your garden centre will advise you.

Just how much you spend depends on your garden size and your pocket. In many cases, however, it is possible to scrounge plants, shrubs and even young, self-seeded trees from friends. In my own case, I could not possibly have bought enough material for my three acres. I was fortunate enough to be given surplus plants and shrubs by friends whose gardens were overgrown, though not all survived transplanting, of course. Another friend had several hundred acres of woodland and I was able to acquire many native trees, like young mountain ash, free of charge. Ask about and you will sooner or later find someone who knows someone who wants rid of something you could make use of.

If your garden is enormous you can fill it with all manner of permutations of trees to give the best nest cover, best berry or seed provision, best singing posts and prettiest appearance. Most gardens, however, are of modest size and owners do not have room for all the trees and shrubs they might like. So with the smaller garden, it is more important than ever to decide beforehand what purpose your trees and shrubs are to serve – from a bird's viewpoint that is. The answer must be that the more limited you are for space, the more you must concentrate on trees and shrubs that give nest cover. Otherwise birds may visit you but cannot nest with you.

Some of the best nest-cover trees have been mentioned earlier. All shrubs and trees and climbing plants also have seeds or berries of some sort and almost all are edible from a bird's viewpoint. All will have insects thriving in their leaves and will provide insect food too. So if you select your trees purely from a nest-cover aspect, these will incidentally offer some amount of insects and berries, seeds or fruits. If you should be short on the food element, you can make this up yourself by means of food offered on your bird table.

Of the trees already mentioned as nest cover priorities, food is also offered by larch, Scots pine, spruce, cypress, holly, ivy, elder, hawthorn, blackthorn and beech. Less cover but more food is offered by birch, mountain ash, ash, alder, oak and, of course, orchard fruit trees.

Obviously it is not all a matter of planting more. Some gardens are so overstocked and choked that they will need to be thinned out drastically before any birds can get into them. Some Victorian gardens are of that nature, packed tight with rhododendrons like small forests. Space is especially important close to the house, where you will want your bird table, for that certainly should not be over-hung with trees or shrubs, as birds may be afraid to come for food when nearby shrubbery may conceal danger. You need space too for your water container, whether a pond or bird-bath, and this is the topic we examine next.

2
Water

IF YOU ARE to have any success in attracting birds, then water is essential. All birds need this to drink and bathe in, some to swim in, and a few to nest on. The bigger the area of water you can arrange, the better. If the size of your garden is such that a pond is out of the question, then a bird-bath will do. The problem is that it must be kept full, and that means topping it up every day, and in winter it will freeze solid. If using a bird-bath of the pedestal type, then ideally it needs to be out of the range of cats. Most cats can easily jump to bird-bath height, so ensure a clear open space for some yards around it so that birds will have ample chance to spot an approaching cat.

A far better idea than a conventional bird-bath would be some shallow vessel such as an upturned dustbin lid sunk into the ground – provided cats can't sneak up to it under cover. This must be shallow towards its edges so that small birds can bathe in it as well as drink from it. It will need flushing regularly, as if the water goes stale and stagnant, the birds will go somewhere else. Small plastic garden ponds can be bought today at no great expense and some of these look prettier than dustbin lids. It is best to set such a pond on to a bedding of gravel to act as a soakaway for surplus water during rain or flushing out with a hose. A larger one will obviously need more to drain it than a little gravel.

There are all manner of permutations in making a pond, however small it might have to be because of restricted space. A hose-pipe from an outside tap can be laid easily and permanently under a lawn, so that it is only a matter of turning on the tap for a few minutes a week to keep the pond full and fresh. If you have the space, then the bigger the pond, the more birds you will attract. A large pond can be a problem if your soil is porous, when it might be necessary to lay down a heavy-duty plastic liner like thick polythene. If you have a source of running water close by, it might be possible to divert a small inflow, either as an open ditch or piped below ground. Such a stream-fed pond will need an outflow too, and a gravel soakaway is unlikely to be adequate, especially in time of flood.

Even a large pond does not have to be deep, unless you particularly want it deep, for instance to keep fish in. If making a large pond, you may need special advice as the stresses from water pressure can be immense, and you may flood out your neighbours. If you build it on sloping ground, then you need worry about damming only the down side. A depth of six inches to one foot is ample for any size of pond designed to attract birds. This is deep enough for any water birds to be able to dabble in. At such a depth you can wade into it in wellington boots for the occasional jobs of maintenance, planting water-lilies or clearing debris. In a deep pond such jobs can become a major undertaking, but great fun.

If you want to keep fish too, then it will have to be deeper, or at least have some areas which are deeper, depending on what fish and how many. A garden pond is hardly likely to exceed a diameter of, say, thirty feet at most. Beyond this we would regard it as a small lake, where other rules apply and you will certainly need specialist advice.

The birds which visit such a pond will be mainly land birds coming to drink and bathe, but any water birds likely to be attracted to it will be of such a size and type as to prove no danger to fish. Moorhens will not bother fish. Dippers might take small fry but are birds of fast water and unlikely to stay more than a few minutes on a still pond. Kingfishers might well take small fish, but if you are lucky enough to have kingfishers visit your pond, you might accept that as a small price to pay. I've seen kingfishers on my pond only two or three times in fifteen years and they were so marvellous to watch, I'd gladly spare them a fish or two. Coots might take small fish, but these are birds of larger ponds than garden size and so are unlikely to be a problem.

In the country herons are the biggest problem and they will grow confident enough to come to ponds even close to houses and some-times even to ponds hemmed in by bushes, which might impede their clumsy getaway. Once they find a source of fish, they will come back time and again till they have the lot. Herons cleared a family of water voles from my pond in a week, spearing them with their bills and swallowing them whole – quite gruesome to watch.

The only defence against herons is to have a pond with vertical sides containing water at least three feet deep. A heron likes to wade in cautiously and will not stride off a vertical bank into deep water. That, at least, is the theory. This would be satisfactory only if you want to protect your golden carp, and a neighbour of mine has such a pond with sheer brick-built sides standing three feet above water level and with water several feet deep, reminiscent of a septic tank with the lid off and about as attractive. I don't know if it frightens herons but looking over the edge certainly frightens me! Such a heron-proof pond is useless for bird gardeners, in so far as no birds can use it either to drink from or bathe in.

One way of protecting your fish from herons is to run nets over the top of the pond. This not only spoils the whole effect but will also deter most smaller birds from going near, and those that do will be in danger of getting trapped in the netting. Neither method seems compatible with a pond designed to attract bird life. The only compromise is to have a pond with one shallow end for bathing birds. The other banks can be deeper with perhaps one very deep area where fish have at least half a chance of avoiding herons. On sloping ground a pond with the deep side running to perhaps a maximum of four feet gives your fish somewhere to escape to beyond a heron's reach, whilst leaving a shallow end for bathing birds. A retaining wall to hold back a four-foot depth of water involves miniature dam-building, so try a smaller pond first till you gain experience. For most gardens, however, herons will not be a problem.

If you have the space and possibilities for water supply and drainage, then the effort and cost of installing a decent-sized pond will be well repaid. Ten feet by twenty should be a good size. Beyond that you may run in to problems of scale, water pressure on bankings, and that of lining the bed of the pond, if your soil is other than clay. A pond of this sort of size attracts all kinds of birds and becomes a central feature of your garden from the point of view not only of bird life but also of water plants, which can grown around it and even on it.

With a pond this size I personally think it is a good idea to keep a few domestic ducks. They will spend much time on the water so that there is always something of interest to watch, and their habits are not incompatible with wild bird life of any kind. As long as you can enclose the area in which you would like them to remain, they can be left out in all weathers and they will live a semi-wild existence. They require no shelter – in fact, if you make one they will probably refuse to use it even in the worst frosts or snow. Most domestic ducks are too fat and too lazy to fly, being considerably larger than the wild equivalent. If they do, then clipping the flight feathers of one wing will stop them for a season.

Ducks are messy creatures and you will need to have them fenced off from your house entrance, where they will otherwise cluster once they learn where the food comes from. One drake is ample for up to half a dozen ducks. A higher proportion than that, and the drakes will be constantly fighting.

Wild birds soon get used to seeing your ducks on the pond, where they do quite literally act as decoys to encourage other birds to come down to what they see is a safe place. We have had the pleasure of seeing a wild mallard duck bring her brood of newly hatched youngsters to our pond, presumably attracted there by the sight of our own ducks. Wild ducks are unlikely to attempt to nest with you unless you have a really large expanse of water or wet meadowland. Domestic ducks will, however, make a nest and hatch our their young if allowed to, which is a most enjoyable event to witness. Bear in mind, though, that each duck may rear a dozen youngsters, and you may very soon be looking for new homes for them by autumn. Our own duck population rose from four to 40 in one particular season, after which we have usually stopped them hatching by removing the eggs daily.

Domestic ducks nesting out in the open (semi-wild) make stupid parents. They may be inclined to start sitting on eggs as early as February or March, which means the young would hatch out far too early in the year and would probably die from excess rain or cold. Mother ducks trail tiny offspring through wet and mud regardless, and young ducklings can very quickly get cold, wet and exhausted and can die within an hour if left. Ducks seem not to notice youngsters which fall by the way, and they wander off with the rest of the brood oblivious to a trail of dying youngsters left behind. Even wild mallard ducks do this, but domestic ducks make far worse parents. To avoid this happening, remove any eggs till about late April. This way, the ducks cannot start brooding till May and the young will hatch out at a time when decent, warmer weather is a possibility.

An exhausted duckling found lying in the mud will often recover amazingly if taken indoors in a box and warmed near a cooker for an hour. A domestic duck will accept the youngster back again an hour later without noticing. A wild mallard duckling found in this way is unlikely to survive and you have no' chance of getting near the mother to return her offspring anyway.

Wild ducks can feed themselves quite happily, but domestic ducks living a semi-wild existence cannot. If you have some, you will need to feed them daily. They eat almost any household scraps, but the simplest thing to give them are the feed pellets they make for chickens, as these contain all the necessary ingredients, including the grit needed for shells, which on some soils they have difficulty in finding.

If possible, try building a small island on your pond. All it needs are a few stones piled together with a little soil on top and a few irises or other vegetation. Many birds may feel inclined to linger there where they feel safe. Domestic ducks will sleep on such an island or on the water itself, where they are generally safe enough from foxes.

A floating island can be a solution for a deep pond. All you need are a few logs or planks nailed together and anchored by tying a couple of stones on to ropes. A little soil on top, together with a few plants, will in no time make the floating island look like the real thing. It can be as small or as large as you please.

Ducks and certain other water birds like to paddle. They will stand, sometimes for long periods, with their feet in the water and their bodies out, so include a small area of submerged stones an inch or two below the surface and well out from the bank.

For 'gardens' large enough to cope with such a pond, the scope is endless because the scale is becoming large enough to simulate nature. In many a garden of more conventional size, a pond thirty feet by ten feet would occupy too much to the garden space. The problem here might not be so much that of finding space for it, but that such a pond might then be hemmed in too closely all round with trees, shrubs and plants. One advantage with a pond, assuming the flow can be controlled satisfactorily and safely in drought as well as in flood, is that water is maintenance free. There are none of the usual garden chores such as grass cutting, leaf gathering, pruning and the rest.

The disadvantage of a pond too big for the garden is that birds will be wary of coming down to it, where too many bushes encroach and their field of vision (and safety) is restricted. I would not suggest filling your garden with water to this degree: better a small pond with some open expanse around it, perhaps of lawn or even a paved area. Most small garden birds will use it for drinking and bathing whatever its size, so long as they feel safe there. Most will come to its edges, not to the water surface itself, so surface area is less important than accessible, shallow-sloping banks.

For those who have the space and enthusiasm to make a larger pond, one problem encountered as soon as it is filled with water is what to plant on and around it, because at first it will look very bare and unattractive. The side closest to the house is best left unplanted so that the observer's field of view is not obstructed. The planting then is going to be on the two sides and the far bank. The taller-growing plants are best sited on the far bank, because not only will they then not block the view of the pond, but also they will there reflect attractively in the surface like a mirror.

Irises make a marvellous backdrop to a pond. There are several colours, commonly yellow and purple. They are hardy, quick-growing, run to about three feet in mid-season, keep some colour in winter, and have the advantage that they will grow in water or on the banking and will spread willingly in both water and soil. You can buy various forms of these from any garden centre and may have to do so to start off with. However, if you know anyone who has a pond you will probably find you can obtain them free, as owners have to thin them out every few years or they soon take over the whole area. They are very easily transplanted and any clump, however carelessly cut or pulled, will soon start growing in its new site. Irises are virtually impossible to kill, so the most unskilled gardener cannot go wrong with them.

Another tall-growing pond plant is commonly called the bulrush but is correctly known as the reedmace. This grows to a height of six feet in mid-season and has a marvellous, large seedhead, which is much loved for flower arranging and eaten by some birds in hard winter weather. It spreads very rapidly and anyone having this plant in a pond will gladly give you some, since its 'walking' habit is such that it will throw up another stem every six inches or so and can travel six feet in a season, mostly walking into the water. It will grow in water (rooting in the bottom mud) or on the banks and is very hardy. It appears very dead in winter but new stems shoot up in spring.

It is less advisable to plant trees or shrubs close to the water's edge, as the leaf spread may encroach too far over the water, and many trees will die if their roots actually grow into water. If you want these as a backdrop to your rushes, then plant them some distance in the background, twice the distance you first thought of.

Don't plant too much too close to the water. Remember that you do need some open, shallow banking where the soil slopes gently into the water, for this is where birds will bathe and drink. This area needs to be encroached by nothing in the way of herbage and it needs to be where you can see it from your house or viewpoint. The left- or right-hand banks are probably the best areas for this bathing slope, ideally where it can face the rising sun. Many birds like to warm up in the early morning sun and this is the spot where the ice is likely to melt first on a hard winter morning.

The most successful ponds for attracting birds are likely to be those which most closely imitate nature. A neat pond with well-kept border plants and a lawn trimmed neatly down to its edge may look well in gardening terms but can be pretty boring to a bird. A semi-wild appearance means there are more nooks and crannies, humps and hollows and interesting corners where birds may find the odd insect or edible greenery. A few half-submerged rough stones near the far bank may mean that tiny water creatures gather there and birds will then spend more time there in searching them out. Many birds will have a two-minute bath and be away again, but a pond where insect life abounds in muddy corners will attract grey wagtails, pied wagtails, wrens and perhaps even dippers as well as more common birds.

Your pond can be on level ground or sloping. Personally I think sloping ground is better, as the shallow (upper) end tapers naturally into the water. In this case, what you are building is actually a kind of dam, the deep end formed by either a bank of soil or a couple of rows of cemented stones, like a low wall. In the end what you do with it is far more important than shape, size or levels. If using a plastic liner, then the surplus overlap can be buried in the topsoil and perhaps held firm with a few rough stones.

If you wish, you can buy varying types of pondweed with which to make the effect more interesting. Nothing is quite as bland as a pond with a bare concrete base or a bare plastic liner. Birds probably find it as boring as we do, as it is essentially unnatural. Some water plants are surface-floating and some root in the mud on the pond bed. Some of the latter are oxygenaters i.e. they put oxygen into the water, which may help to keep it clear and fresh. Your local garden centre will advise on these if asked. It is possible that oxygenaters alone will not be adequate to fully freshen the water, and this is especially important if you hope to keep a few fish in it. So even with such plants, you may still need to freshen the water by running a hose for a few minutes a week, and also to top up the level in dry weather. Ducks will dig out bottom-rooted plants unless you surround their roots with stones, and even then they will enjoy trying.

Try to beg a few plants from other pond owners, who usually end up with an excess. I would also forget about oxygenaters and accept that you have to freshen up the water regularly, if you are unable to keep a constant flow-through of water. Bubbling water puts its own oxygen in as it flows. Naturally-occurring water plants will probably prove hardier than cultivated and are probably much cheaper. Someone once bought me a very expensive water-lily for my pond. I never saw a sign of it after three days, but my ducks really enjoyed it. Ducks seem to hardly bother eating natural wild plants – of course, if they're starving, they will. If they do, it doesn't really matter, as natural, wild plants spread quicker than they can eat them.

Geese look nice on a pond and enjoy swimming. If you have geese, they will bully the ducks and eat all your water plants and still be hungry. When you get geese, you're a farmer not a gardener.

Sooner or later, tiny water creatures will find their way into your pond. If you want to speed this up by introducing frogspawn, water snails, beetles etc, then by all means do. You can buy some of these from specialist suppliers or you can try bringing home a bottle of water from a natural stream each time you go into the country, as this will contain larvae of all kinds. Some water creatures will eat others and eventually your pond will find a happy equilibrium. Give your larvae a chance to develop by not hosing the pond out fiercely and entirely like washing the car. Be cautious about putting such things as frogspawn into a new pond in a small garden, as you may create a sudden imbalance of nature and find yourself knee-deep in frogs.

You can put as much or as little effort in to a pond as you feel happy with. Make it your life's work or do it in an afternoon. The whole point of it is to have a pond you can enjoy, which will attract bird life. If you make it a rod for your own back, then it will cease to bring the pleasure it ought. If it is big enough, you can paddle in it in your wellies, dig in the mud and get really dirty on your day off!

I suggest you forget about spirit levels and concrete mixing, unless, of course, you are a do-it-yourself enthusiast, when you will derive great pleasure from this side of the job. All you need in the end is a hole in the ground that will hold water, a supply of water to it, and a drain or soakaway for an overflow. Water finds its own level and birds don't know or care whether a bank is level or sloping, as long as it has a shallow shore area they can drink and bathe in.

If you do decide to make a pond, for heaven's sake put it where you can see it from the house, if at all possible. There is always something happening on or beside a pond, especially early in the morning. If you can see it from your house window, you will derive pleasure from it every single day, even if only during breakfast, and the programme is far more interesting than Breakfast TV. I'm very fortunate as my area of boggy and useless, low-lying land adapted easily into a series of five small ponds, which overflow into one another and the land happened to have a natural clay content, so that simply digging holes was enough without any lining problems.

3
Enemies of Birds

GREY SQUIRRELS ARE charming creatures which soon become very confident and tame. They will come regularly and readily to bird tables or to the house window to feed on almost anything from food scraps to peanuts and will even learn to feed from your hand. They are extremely agile and will easily run or clamber along a clothes-line when they need to. Their antics make them very endearing and amusing to watch. Unfortunately they are vicious killers, expert at finding nests, and will eat every egg and nestling they can find. They will also eat strawberries and gooseberries and, once they find a clump, will clear the whole harvest within days.

Each year many of our early nests are destroyed as eggs or young are taken by grey squirrels, despite the fact that I shoot as many as I can. They can even gnaw their way into nest boxes if they have a mind to, though usually blue tits and other box nesters are safe from them as long as the box timber is of reasonable thickness. If you have the problem of squirrels gnawing their way into best boxes, the solution is to tack a metal cover, cut from a piece of tin or brass, round the hole, which will deter them, though I have even seen them gnaw their way through the wire mesh of a peanut feeder to get at the nuts.

Most people know that squirrels are vermin, but are charmed by their endearing appearance and their tameness, and, as they don't actually witness the robbing of nests, they dismiss this unpleasant side of their nature from their minds. I once watched helplessly as one raided a moorhen's nest in a cluster of reeds on my own pond, despite the pitiful attempts by the birds at driving it off, and my own futile attempts at shooting it in the act, as it was hidden by the dense reeds. It returned time and again till within a day it had cleared the entire clutch of eggs, even carrying and rolling away those it could not eat on the spot.

The only solution to the squirrel problem is to shoot them, drastic though this may seem to those concerned to try to preserve wildlife, and even if, like myself, you feel terrible pangs of guilt when you kill one. Those householders who do not have a gun or live in a town situation do not have this remedy available. For them, all I can suggest is that on no account should they do anything to encourage them, and this means making sure the food put out for birds cannot be reached by squirrels. They will eat anything birds eat and persistently raid bird tables. As squirrels are agile climbers and can jump across most gaps they cannot climb across, this is easier said than done. A bird table which stands on a single-stem post and has a very wide overlap at the top may just defeat hem, provided it is high enough from the ground to prevent them jumping on to it. A round iron post makes climbing up it hard work. The problem then is that the bird table may be sited in such a position that it cannot be viewed from the house window.

Squirrels are sometimes a problem even in the middle of cities where shooting may be impractical and where sometimes they will even nest in roof areas under house eaves. Once they get into the loft they can do terrible damage to such things as lead pipes and electric wiring, and a phone call to the local authority pest control department may well produce some remedies.

The native red squirrel is said to be far less harmful to bird life, though it is known to take eggs. The red should not be confused with the grey, though the latter has a gingery tint to its grey coat in the breeding season. If it is stealing eggs, then we don't really care what colour it is. Red squirrels, however, are protected and must not be shot. Red squirrels are not common everywhere nowadays, being driven out by the stronger greys. In my own area of North Yorkshire I have not seen one in 25 years.

Cats are natural enemies of birds and will stalk and kill them just for fun. One way to keep neighbouring cats from a garden is to keep a dog. Dogs wander harmlessly about a garden, and, though they might chase after the odd blackbird on the lawn just for fun, they have no chance of catching it. Dogs will do no harm to your birds.

This is the only redress you have against a neighbour's cat, which is protected under the law although its owner is not responsible for its actions under the law, as a dog owner might be. It is virtually impossible to make a fence that will keep a cat out of your garden, though you could make a determined effort. You can try cat repellents such as are sold commercially, especially at the place you believe cats may enter your garden. My own garden is troubled by cats from neighbouring farms, as many as half a dozen sometimes, and some will come from almost a mile away. I've found that vinegar and/or pepper on their usual routes is definitely not popular, but they just find a different way round.

If you are plagued by cats, then it is a problem with no real solution. Try to avoid encouraging low-nesting birds, as cats are less troublesome to birds nesting higher than about five feet. They can climb, of course. If cats are inclined to try climbing a tree where you know there is a nest, maybe some dead bramble stems wound round the trunk a few times will deter them, or a few holly clippings tied to the trunk.

Rats are not so much a problem in town gardens as in the country, not usually anyway. However, if there are rats in the neighbourhood and you leave food out where they can reach it, then you will have them as regular visitors – even though they might come mostly at night and you will be unaware of their presence. In the country they are more of a problem, especially near farms, as most farms have rats. Many farmers accept than as an inevitable part of farming, usually because there are stores of feed constantly available.

Rats are not quite as agile as grey squirrels but are good climbers, all the same. They can often climb a sheer wall by taking a running jump at it. A good high bird table with a wide overhang may well defeat them, but they will certainly find ground food and come regularly for it. They will take not only food but birds' eggs and young birds too.

You can try shooting them if you happen to spot them, but they don't usually linger at feeding places in daylight, so seldom does the opportunity arise. Poison is the likeliest answer. Put poison (your chemist will sell it) in a known rat hole and cover it with a stone to keep it away from birds. If you can't find a rat hole, put it under a stone is some corner where you have seen or suspect rats, again under a stone. Some rat poison contains wheat seeds and birds will probably eat it if they see it.

Rats very soon become immune to poison. If you give them a little bit regularly, they soon get used to it and come back for more till it becomes part of their daily intake. If you suspect rats, the thing to do is give them a good big dose straight away. Give them a big pile. They will east it greedily for a day or two. When you see they have stopped eating it, they're probably dead or dying. Rats are not a pretty sight at the the best of times, but a dying rat is a most repulsive thing. Not to go into too gruesome detail, it is a fact that rats dying from poison will usually come into daylight because they go blind, a deliberate effect of the poison. The reason is that a rat that dies under your floorboards or in a hidden place will smell most appallingly for many days. So a poisoned rat can be seen in daylight staggering about helplessly, when bolder birds will attack it and create a general disturbance because of its presence. If that happens it's up to you to put it out of its misery by a blow from a heavy stick. Don't try to pick it up; it may bite you.

From all this, you can see that you are far better off without rats in the first place. Don't put food where they can get it, and you'll probably never see one.

Magpies are the most troublesome members of the crow family in terms of the harm they do to bird life. Pretty well most members of the crow family will eat eggs, some even nestlings, given the chance. Jackdaws and rooks may even invade a hen-run once they get a taste for hen eggs, but they are not normally very troublesome to wild birds. Carrion crows are said to be keen nest finders, but I've never found them to be a problem myself. Compared to the magpie, the rest of the crow family are just beginners. The magpie is nest hunting most of the time and many early nests in my own garden are lost through their persistent watching and following of nesting birds till they discover the nest. Once they find a nest, they will return repeatedly till it is emptied of eggs and young.

There is little one can do about this short of shooting them, which is quite legal as they are classed as vermin. They are, however, extremely wily birds and will fly off at the least motion. They very soon learn what a gun is, and just raising one's arms as if to aim a gun will usually scare them off. This is a quite surprising talent as even young birds learn to take fright in this way. I have seen a silhouette scarecrow of a man holding a raised gun made in such a way that it pivots with the wind in the manner of a weather-vane. This might be a solution to magpies and crows, but it's a lot of trouble to go to. In populous areas they may well become more used to people anyway and less likely to take fright in this way.

One step that can be taken against them is to destroy any nest as soon as they start building but that will merely drive them to nest elsewhere nearby, until they have built and succeeded in rearing a brood. A better step for those who are patient and good climbers is to wait till the full clutch of eggs (five to nine) has been laid – usually that means mid- to late April – then remove all the eggs but one. That way the brood reared will be a maximum of one, and the population in the immediate area may slowly reduce over a few years. To remove all the eggs is pointless, as the birds will build again elsewhere and lay again till they rear a brood – this time a full brood. Whilst it is, of course, against the law to take the eggs of most wild birds, magpies are an exception, being regarded as destructive.

This may sound like heartless advice for those who love birds, and I must admit I don't carry it through myself. On the other hand, if you take no steps to discourage them, then magpies may find a small garden sanctuary to be no more than a concentration of easy meals.

On the whole, there is little you can do about magpies except scare them off whenever you see them, so that they may learn they are not welcome in your garden. A clap of the hands will usually do the trick, as it probably reminds them of a gunshot. It won't stop them coming but they might prefer to go elsewhere, where no one bothers to scare them off.

We have only one pair of magpies within flying distance of our garden, but as an indication of their destructiveness, let me point out that so far this year (I wrote this in May) they have taken a clutch of six grey wagtail eggs, five of pied wagtail, eight of pheasant, two of woodpigeon, one of moorhen, three of mallard, a nestful of five nestling bullfinches and a nestful of uncounted willow warbler nestlings.

Foxes are likely to be a problem only to such water birds as ducks. There is little you can do to stop a fox. Provide your water birds with an island. It may not stop a determined fox but it will certainly mean the birds have warning of its approach, and they can move much faster round water than a fox can.

Foxes notoriously stalk their quarry on windy nights, when the sound of their approach is covered by rustling grasses or branches. I only once lost a bird to a fox and that was on a windy night – a goose, in fact. I found the body headless the next day. A fox that has killed will often make off with just the head and may come back later for the rest. Some farmers will take advantage of that fact to poison the carcass, but I'm not suggesting you try that as other carrion eaters may get to it before the fox does. So if you find a headless corpse in your garden, you have foxes. There's not much you can do about it, but keep your dustbin lid tight shut, as they will forage in dustbins, especially in towns. It's a matter of live and let foxes live.

Weasels can also be a pest and will rob nest boxes by climbing inside. If you find out how to stop them, let me know. Jays rob nests too, but I don't know a way of stopping them either.

4
Food

EVERY BIRD GARDENER will want a bird table, a tray of some sort on which to put food. It can be as simple or as complicated as you like. All you need basically is some sort of flat surface on which to place food at some height above ground, ideally a height which may deter cats and squirrels, though height alone will not stop them altogether. Bird tables are usually made of wood, though they don't have to be. At one house I had a large stone roof slate set on top of a stone pedestal formed from a fortunately shaped lintel. It was rain-proof, windproof, rotproof, easy to hose down, and will probably last for ever.

Anyone can make one from any flat piece of wood and a suitable post. A raised lip round three sides of the table top helps to stop food blowing off in breezy weather. One side is best left open to that it can occasionally be scraped clean – though the open side always turns out to be the one where the wind blows food off! The side to leave open is the side you will view it from out of your window or your most frequent observation point. That way you see the whole of each bird on the table, not just its top half.

Where do you site the bird table? It depends on your reason for putting it there in the first place. If your aim is to nourish as many birds as possible, put it in the safest place there is from a bird's point of view, which probably means in a wide open area in the centre of the garden on top of a twenty-foot pole. But I'm sure that's not what you had in mind. Apart from anything else, you'd have to call out the fire brigade whenever you wanted to top up the food. I pointed out this ridiculous extreme to illustrate that this is probably not your real reason for having a bird table in the first place.

What most people want to do is to have the pleasure of watching birds come down to the table to feed. At the same time, you don't want to lure them down to their deaths from predators. So your table needs to be sited as close to your viewpoint (probably a window) as is consistent with safety. How close that is depends on your house condition and how many cats you keep. Cats and birds generally don't get on, and even the most charming cats will maim, kill and eat birds if they get half a chance.

If this happens in the nesting season, it probably means young birds will starve to death in the nest as the surviving parent fails in its attempt to feed the brood alone. There are few sights quite so terrible as a nest full of dead fledglings, although you may be spared this sight personally by failing to come across the nest. Nevertheless, you will be responsible for this unless you do your best to ensure your bird table is as far as possible out of the reach of cats. By setting up a bird table you may be gambling with birds' lives, and that is a responsibility to be taken seriously.

Cats are great companions, but a cat owner who also wants to encourage birds to the garden is in a moral dilemma. Is there really any point in saving the lives of half a dozen birds by providing food for them in harsh weather when your cat has probably eaten that many for breakfast in the same period? It's a difficult one to face up to, so most cat owners don't.

Not many cats will jump six feet into the air nor shin up a sheer bird table post, especially one made from an old metal pipe. Those are the best precautions a cat owner can take, and also to ensure that the table is not overlooked by low-hanging branches from nearby trees, from which acrobatic cats might leap.

If you have no cats, then you have a better chance of siting your bird table where you can get agood view of any activity on it – provided you can manage to keep your neighbour's cat away without poisoning it. You can buy various preparations today intended to keep cats away – the RSPB sells one. Presumably these smell bad to cats. I've tried some of them but they never seemed to work for long, if at all. Probably the effect is diluted or washed away by rain. Vinegar works for a while, and pepper, and might be worth using to protect a low nest for a fortnight till the young fly off.

Ideally you might like your bird table close to your favourite window or the one you most often have a chance to look through. In theory there is no reason why you can't fix the table to the window sill itself, and some are on sale which adhere to the glass. Personally I think this is not a good idea. Birds are messy eaters and will splatter your window all the time. More important is the fact that in excited aerial chases birds often fail to see glass until it is too late, and will frequently crash into windows and kill themselves by breaking their necks. Conservatories are very prone to this because of the sheer volume of glass.

At two o'clock one morning my burglar alarms were set off by an almighty thump on a window. Investigating cautiously outside

I found a very dazed tawny owl rocking on its haunches below the window. Fortunately it had recovered and gone by breakfast time. If owls with their keen sight can fail to see glass, small birds are much more prone to it. Over the years we have had fatalities after crashing into glass windows from the following species: song thrush, blackbird, blue tit, great tit, coal tit, nuthatch, goldcrest, chiffchaff, hedge sparrow, robin, chaffinch and probably others I can't remember. Some are simply dazed and recover after an hour, but most die instantly. We have tried all kind of remedies against this, such as hanging hawk silhouettes against the glass, but nothing seems to prevent it. Most incidents occur early in the morning when birds are careering about recklessly. If this happens under normal conditions, then putting a feed table up against a glass window is asking for trouble.

In any event, many birds will be too timid to come down to feed on a table on a window sill. Perhaps if you live alone and sit quietly, they might. But many a normal household filled with noisy children and disco music may not be entirely conducive.

The solution for most of us is a bird table far enough away from the window to attract birds and yet still give us a good view of the proceedings. For most situations this means about six feet from the window, and set at a height that gives optimum visibility – bearing in mind the cat problem. The commoner and more confident birds will come this close readily. Those which are more nervous or shy, like woodpeckers, will do so only hesitantly and will take off at the slightest sign of movement from within the house – at least mine always do. A table this close to the house is less troublesome to keep replenished, especially in bad weather.

A flat table top is adequate, indeed in some respects preferable, as birds will not be anxious about coming into a confined space under a roof. A table with a roof, on the other hand, has the advantage that the food and feeders are kept dry. If you opt to buy a bird table rather than make your own, then to some extent your choice is determined by what is on offer. In the end it makes little difference whether you have a roof or not, except in snow, though with a roof larger birds will be impeded and will probably not use it – such birds as rooks, jackdaws and pheasants. Though we may not think of these larger birds as typical bird-table visitors, they will come on to it on occasion, clumsy though they may be.

A food table should be just that and nothing else. By this I mean you should not attempt to incorporate a nest box into it (see page 39). I would also suggest not combining it with a bird-bath. This is because a dominant bird or two will drive others off while it eats or bathes, so with birds that do that, your viewing is limited to one bird at a time – feeding, bathing or drinking. Having a separate water point means you have two chances of observing birds at the same time and avoids constant bickering between the hungry, the thirsty and the dirty. The same goes for a peanut feeder, which is an essential item. No harm is done by having one attached to your bird table if you feel like it, but to position it somewhere else nearby and still within your field of vision gives you an extra chance for bird visitors.

Obviously you will make your own decision as to whether to have bird-bath, table and nut feeder all in one, or as three separate items set some distance apart. If you are keen to photograph birds and want to set up your camera and tripod at the ready, ideally with a long cable release so that you can be well back from their view, then you might want to site all three together, as that way you will have three times the chance of getting something to photograph at any one time and in the right spot. If your interest is just to be able to watch birds as they feed, then by splitting these three items apart, you have three separate chances that there will be something to watch at any one time.

What to feed the birds with? You can do it expensively by buying every possible mixture of food and seed known to attract anything from escaped budgerigars to mute swans. Or you can do it cheaply by offering nothing but household waste and scapes. It is up to you.

I think the one essential item apart from household scraps is a peanut feeder. You can, of course, thread unshelled peanuts on to a string and watch the amusing antics of birds trying to get the nuts out. If you propose using unshelled peanuts, then a wire is better than a string, as one end will stab straight through the nut-with-shell and the other can be formed into a hook to hang from wherever you choose. Personally I don't use unshelled nuts. When I did, I found that I never seemed to have time to thread them and birds went for days without nuts until I remembered or found time. Another reason, however, is that once the bird gets through the husk to the nut, it usually flies off with it to eat it somewhere out of sight, and I don't feel I've had my money's worth.

With a peanut feeder, the shelled nuts are enclosed in a wire mesh and the birds have to eat them on site, or nibble them till they are small enough to steal through the grid. A full peanut feeder lasts a lot longer than a string of unshelled nuts and provides better entertainment, though clearly the nuts cost a bit more. A mesh feeder can be bought for as little as two or three pounds.

There are all kinds of peanut feeders, some designed to swing about on a string from a branch, some to be nailed solidly to a post or bird table. Some are all-round mesh, some are wooden with mesh just at the front side. If you use the wooden-sided type, they are open to attack from squirrels who may gnaw through the softwood side to get at the nuts rather than try to gnaw through the mesh – though they are capable of doing that too, if they have a mind to. Also I have had woodpeckers peck through the wooden sides of one to get access rather than put up with trying to peck nuts through the mesh, though most woodpeckers accept the mesh as intended. If you are not troubled with squirrels or woodpeckers, then I would use this wooden-sided type myself. With only one side of mesh, you can control exactly where the birds will come to eat. If you angle the mesh side to the left or right as seen from your viewpoint, you will see the birds eating in full profile rather than the back view of birds you would get if you fixed it with the mesh facing you. If you want to photograph the feeders, then angle the mesh to face your most sunlit side or you'll be taking pictures in shadow.

If you use the all-mesh type, there is a greater than one-in-four chance that the birds will feed on the side you can't see, that is the side furthest from your window, where they perhaps feel safer than they do on view. So again you are paying for the entertainment without getting it. If the mesh feeder is hung on a string, it can spin round constantly and again the birds will keep turning into and out of view as it spins. This is particularly annoying if you want to take photographs of the birds as they feed, while a fixed one-sided mesh type means you can pre-set your focus and have a known frame for your subject to appear in.

You might think a nut feeder swinging on a piece of string was safer from squirrels. Perhaps this is marginally true but determined squirrels can climb down a string just as they can up a pole. Nuts will be eaten by all the usual nut eaters, including siskins and nuthatches, but other birds also develop a taste for them. Hedge sparrows and robins will pick up nut crumbs. Chaffinches will occasionally learn to 'hover' long enough to get a beakful of nuts from a feeder, though they are not very good at it. Nuthatches will always head the pecking order of small birds at a nut feeder as no other bird will argue with that respected beak. A woodpecker, of course, is in a class of its own.

Half a coconut, hanging upside down so that it can't collect water, has become a traditional way of feeding nuts to agile birds such as titmice. By hanging it upside down from a piece of string, less agile birds can't get at it, but nimbler ones can, including virtually all the nut eaters you may want to attract. When the half coconut shell is empty you can wedge it firmly into some ivy on a wall and it might make a nesting site for such birds as flycatchers, robins or wagtails.

I have tried coconut feeding and it works fine, but in my opinion a peanut feeder achieves just the same result with a lot less effort. I've also tried fixing up half coconut shells, but nothing ever nested in them.

If you fancy a coconut yourself and can't eat it all, then give half to the birds. But for practical, everyday bird feeding, someone has to buy it, drill it for draining and stringing, saw it in half without cutting fingers, keep the second half somewhere till the first half is eaten, and so on. With peanuts you can keep a bag handy and just top up the mesh feeder as needed. It's not so much a matter of being too lazy to do all this coconut sawing, but in the reality of everyday life, where dashing to work and back takes priority over most things, then coconut sawing falls low on the agenda, gets forgotten or postponed, and then your birds, who have come to rely on you as a food source, go hungry.

Feeding birds by whatever means should be a consistent business. By feeding, you will slowly attract a population of birds which is larger than your garden would support under normal conditions. As long as you keep the food coming, no harm is done. But a stop-go attitude leaves birds hungry when they most need food, and can bring about starvation for birds who might quite happily have survived elsewhere but for your interference. I can think of a number of gardens where owners had a sudden burst of enthusiasm and bought numerous feeding devices and bird attracting toys, which after a couple of weeks were left empty and forgotten and have swung like skeletons in the wind ever since.

So if you live a busy, dash-about sort of life, pick the system of feeding which requires least effort from you and which you are least likely to forget to replenish. The birds will be grateful to you, anyway. If you are going to do it, then do it. But if you are going to be a hit-and-miss bird gardener, then it's probably kinder to birds if you let well alone.

In terms of household waste, most cooked foods will be eaten by some species or another, as will most edible fruit peelings, cores, or fruits that have gone off unexpectedly early. Fruit peelings are best cut into small pieces, when thrushes and blackbirds will usually make off with them. Boiled vegetables, especially potatoes, will be eaten by many species of birds. It is always best to put food out in the morning when it has a chance to be consumed before night. After dark cats and rats and other scavengers may be attracted to it, and birds certainly will not be eating during the hours of darkness.

If you put down food for ground feeders such as thrushes, black-birds, moorhens etc, it is especially important not to leave food down overnight or rats will certainly find it. Rats seldom inhabit an area unless food is available. Leave food down and you'll attract them. The best policy with all bird food (other than that in hoppers and feeders) is to put down only enough to be eaten that day before dark. Birds who miss out by being slow will soon learn to come down sooner. Before long, birds will be waiting for their daily feed.

Those who want to buy special seeds for finches or other selected birds can do so, as all manner of seeds are available from bird food suppliers, some of whom are listed below. I discovered by chance that many birds like chicken meal, nowadays often sold in the form of small pellets as it is less likely to blow away in a wind or be scattered by hens searching for bigger pieces. I feed my chickens and ducks in a ground trough every morning, just enough to last them the day. Many birds, including moorhens, regard this as their food too, and come for it as soon as my back is turned, or even before. Pheasants can't wait for it. Some of 'my' pheasants have become as tame as farmyard poultry. One cock pheasant even learned to tap on the house door if I was late.

Robins and hedge sparrows will regularly peck the smaller pieces from it, as will chaffinches and even blackbirds. This meal is carefully balanced to contain those ingredients essential for a healthy chicken diet, so small birds must know a good thing when they find it. You can crush some into meal for delicate eaters if you wish. A half-hundredweight sack costs about five pounds and lasts for 25 years – well, a long time anyway!

Once breeding gets well under way, say early May, there is usually sufficient insect life to make feeding simple for most birds. Even most seed eating birds feed their young on insects, not seeds. At this time ease off on the artificial food. By the time autumn approaches the harvest of berries arrives. In my own garden birds have first run at blackberries, gooseberries, raspberries, including wild ones, and blackcurrants. Any of these can be planted out in the wild or semi-wild part of the garden and left.

A great many trees and shrubs in your garden will themselves provide food for some species or other in the form of berries and seeds and cones. So will a great many flowers and weeds. So a garden stocked with a good number of these will to some degree take care of a lot of feeding you might otherwise have to provide. In a small garden you may have room for only a limited number of these, and you may well wish to provide seeds in a hopper. Personally I don't put out seed for any of my garden birds, but then I have an unusually large garden with many varieties of trees, including some very ancient trees by the boundary, and mature trees provide not only seeds but whole hordes of insects. I have also a great many weeds, including dandelions, docks and nettles – all great seed providers.

For those who want to buy seeds, the following are suppliers: John E. Haith Ltd, Park Street, Cleethorpes, South Humberside DN35 7NF – several different mixtures of wild bird food are available including seeds and peanuts. Send for a leaflet.

Don't forget the lawn as a source of food. If your lawn is like a billiard table and immaculately free from weeds, it may be the envy of your neighbours, but birds won't thank you for it. Wagtails may gather insects all day from a lawn, as will many birds when feeding young. But if you've eradicated the weeds with chemicals, you've probably also wiped out whole populations of insects which birds would otherwise have eaten. Worse still, the birds may pick up poisoned insects and feed them to their young. What is more, there probably won't be a 'weed' surviving to give any seed eating birds half a chance.

On a fine Tuesday in early May this year I mowed what I refer to as my 'lawn', but what real gardeners would probably think was a piece of rough meadowland. I always cut it on the highest setting, which leaves a green appearance but doesn't clip off everything just above the roots. Grass forms only a proportion of my lawn, which has never seen any chemicals. Clover and dandelions make up a fair percentage, but they all look green when they're cut. On Wednesday the dandelion heads stood proud again. On Friday greenfinches and linnets were having a merry breakfast on the dandelion seeds while the dew was still wet. Pied wagtails and grey wagtails were picking out insects and swallows swooped low across the grass gathering up insects as they flew past. My lawn is there so that I can enjoy it, but part of that enjoyment is in seeing the birds enjoying it too.

5
Nest Boxes

BY PROVIDING NEST boxes for our garden birds, what we are attempting to do is to provide them with alternative sites to make up for deficiencies in nature, and to provide those sites, conveniently for us, within our own gardens. The enclosed type of nest box, such as that used by titmice, is a substitute for a natural nest hole, which hole nesters would once have found in ancient trees or perhaps in rock faces. Today woodlands are often smaller than in the past, and old and declaying trees may have been weeded out or logged for firewood. So the natural availability of tree hole nest sites has declined and is probably still declining. Many modern plantations are of conifers and are felled before the decaying stage.

The open-fronted type of nest box varies from a mere shallow tray with a rim round the edge (as sometimes put out for spotted flycatchers) to a complete box with the front half-open, often used to attract robins. This open-fronted box attempts to compensate birds for lost natural sites which would have existed as ledges, nooks, hollows and crannies in rock faces, soil bankings, and so on, at a time when far more wild places existed in the form of uncultivated corners.

Each species of bird probably has its own personal preference for a certain kind of site within its own category. With hole nesters, for instance, a blue tit may have different preferences from a pied flycatcher or a starling. In providing boxes for these birds today, we are limited as to how much variation we can provide, so we try to average out the requirements of birds as far as we understand them and obviously our understanding of them is limited anyway. Apart from varying the size of the box itself, we do this by making the entrance hole of such a size as to admit birds we aim to encourage and to exclude those we don't. This is the only practical way we can plan exclusively. If we want to encourage blue tits and not starlings, we have to be sure the hole is small enough to keep out the latter and ideally any other unwanted smaller birds too, such as house sparrows.

For blue tits, as for most hole nesters, there is an optimum hole size – details for each species are given under the notes on page 68. If you want blue tits in your garden and nothing else, then plan boxes on that dimension only. In practice, however, we want to encourage not only blue tits but all kind of other hole nesters too, with a few possible exceptions, such as perhaps starlings. So in reality we compromise. We make the boxes large enough to cope with the biggest of the hole nesters we want to attract, and the hole size big enough to admit the largest desired species. And if we do this, then exactly which size of hole is ideal for which bird becomes of no more than academic interest, because we are going to admit the lot, excluding the undesirables as far as we can.

Which species you regard as undesirable depends on where you live and what species might be regarded as a nuisance there. For instance, house sparrows are regarded by many as unwelcome and bird gardeners often plan their boxes to exclude them. There are enough house sparrows in the world for them not to need our assistance and they tend to bully other birds of similar size and take over the choice sites at the expense of other birds. However, in my own garden we hardly ever see a house sparrow and so I can plan my own boxes without having any regard to hole sizes which exclude them.

For your own garden you can plan according to your local conditions, unless you buy standard boxes, when you will have to accept the hole size chosen for you by the makers (or enlarge it, if you wish). For all practical purposes we mostly want to include all smaller birds, perhaps accepting house sparrows as inevitable if we have to. The hole size which will accommodate all smaller hole nesting birds is found by drawing a pencil round a tenpenny piece (1⅛-inch diameter), which will produce a hole just under 1¼-inches in diameter.

This 1¼-inch maximum might just admit house sparrows but will also admit the bigger of the desirable hole nesters, namely pied fly-catchers and nuthatches, whilst at 1⅛-inches these latter two species might have to struggle to get in. Starlings need a two inch hole. No other birds except woodpeckers need anything above the 1¼-inch maximum unless you want to attract such birds as jackdaws or stock doves. Bear in mind that if you try anything with a jackdaw size of hole (six-inch diameter), the box will admit grey squirrels, who will eat any contents, eggs or young. If woodpeckers want to take over your boxes they will enlarge the hole to the size they want anyway.

Grey squirrels are quite capable of gnawing their way into a box by enlarging an entrance hole, but if the wood is of reasonable thickness, they will get bored before they succeed. I once made one from one-inch pulpboard, which, after a season in the weather, they gnawed through in minutes, but fortunately the box was unoccupied at the time. Take warning that pulpboard is unsuitable as a material as it softens when rained on.

Boxes can be made from any old scrap timber you have to hand, but ideally not less than half an inch thick. Three-quarters of a inch is better and will last longer. It may be tempting to use thin wood in the haste to get on with the job, but a year or two later you will regret it and have to start all over again, so in the end it is better to get it right first time. Internal floor dimensions of four inches by four will suit any of these smaller box nesters, but I always think five by five is better. Better too big than too small as, if need be, the birds will pack more nest material in to take up the excess.

Birds are not fussy about the quality of craftsmanship, and have no preference for peaked roofs or sloping ones, side entrance holes or front ones. Just make it as waterproof and as free from draughts as you can. Some like a drainage hole or two in the base to let rain-water drain off should any get in. With my own boxes, I usually try to cover the roof with some waterproof material – there are various plastics or roofing felt materials about today and any old leftover bits of such stuff will add years to your box life. A surplus lino tile can be just the job – if too bright, then paint it dull. I happen to have been lucky enough to have had some old bits of lead flashing material left from a builder's job, and covered the roof of my boxes in lead. This makes a perfect job but we have to watch out for thieves stealing lead from a lot of small roofs!

Of course, you can vary the size and design to suit your own preferences, always bearing in mind the essential requirements of the birds you seek to accommodate. Enclosed nest boxes of this type have a high occupation rate, the highest of any type of nest box and sometimes within a very short time of erecting the box, though more often after a season out in the weather has given the box the look of natural timber. Boxes should be fixed up by February to have a good chance of being used that season, but I have had boxes set up as late as April occupied within days. If you are anxious to get on with it, then set your nest box up regardless of the time of year rather than leave it in waiting for the right time. The right time is right now!

Birds do have a preference for detached bungalows rather than semis or blocks of flats. By this I mean that one sometimes sees ingenious bird gardeners who have made a two-storey box with the idea of inviting one pair of birds to occupy each floor. This may seem a good idea but is not. In practice birds will get confused and may start to build in both boxes, finishing neither nest. Alternatively two pairs of the same species will squabble as they will not normally accept such close proximity of neighbours.

The question of how many boxes to a given area is one I don't think can be answered, as conditions and the species of birds present vary so greatly. I've read that one should err on the side of too few boxes rather than too many, but personally I can't see the point in that. If you're going to do it, do it! Birds can't nest in boxes you don't erect. Certainly don't put them too close together, nor more than one on any particular tree or post. Adjacent boxes may be occupied by the same or different species and you cannot tell in advance of the birds moving in. A pair of birds will be less tolerant of another pair of the same species nearby, while they may totally ignore a pair of a different species. Assume a ten-yard gap between boxes is the minimum privacy distance and see how you get on – that is, between boxes of the same type, but you may intersperse enclosed boxes with open-fronted ones at closer intervals than that.

Enclosed nest boxes usually have a higher occupancy rate than the tray type or open-fronted ones we shall look at next. But sometimes the birds totally ignore them, or examine them and then reject them. Are there any reasons for this? Is there something about a particular box which puts birds off? Well, here are a few suggestions.

With a new box you have a choice of whether to stain it, creosote it, paint it with gloss paint or leave it in raw wood, it should make no difference in theory, though the box may have to weather a week or two to let the smell wear off. My own feeling is that the natural site we are trying to imitate would be raw wood and raw wood should appeal more to a bird's instincts than something stained or painted. So my natural inclination is towards an untreated box. Having said that, a new box in 'white' wood stands out on a tree like a sore thumb – tree barks are grey, black or green (except for birch, and birch trunks are seldom thick enough to carry a box anyway). The elements will turn a white wood box green in two or three years, but in the meantime it looks quite out of place to us and perhaps also to birds.

I usually treat my boxes with a dark-coloured stain, not to proof them against weather but to make them match their surroundings more. More recently I have painted them in khaki green gloss. My occupied boxes have usually been those which have been out in the weather a couple of years and have gone a natural green colour or one which I coloured dark to begin with. But is the reason for occupancy the colour, the position, the angle or just a fortunate spot in the garden? Only the birds know.

The site of a box may well have a bearing on its being occupied. How high should you set it? For all the hole nesting birds we are likely to attract in enclosed boxes (see list on page 47) none needs have a box higher than six feet or lower than three. Most birds are adaptable within reason and a height of between four and six feet is one which is convenient for you to reach in fixing, inspecting and maintaining, and suits the birds too. There may be reasons, however, why this height might not suit your particular garden – the presence of cats or inquisitive children, for instance – and in that case you may want to site the boxes higher, say between six and twelve feet up, and this should make little difference to your occupation rate. Nothing is to be gained by climbing 25-feet up a tree to fix your box – quite the opposite, as this is an unnatural height for most of these birds.

You can fix your box to a tree, a fence post, a wall – in fact, anything that will hold it. Birds do seem to particularly like a box on top of a tree trunk, such as a stump which stands alone at about the right height. If you are clearing unwanted trees, it is a good idea to saw the tree off at a height of about six feet and fix a nest box on top of the remaining stump. This probably simulates a natural decayed stump of a fallen tree, which may have been likely to have nest holes. It may also be something to do with the safe field of view from an isolated stump in an otherwise open clearing. With some species of tree such as willow and ash, new growth will sprout from the sawn-off stump, forming a kind of protective foliage above the nest box. If you have the chance of a log six feet or so in length and want to go to the trouble, you could 'plant' it eighteen inches or so into the ground and fix your box on top of that. A heavy, round fence post (larch lasts longest) of perhaps six inches in diameter or more would do the job just as well as a thicker log. This kind of stump box is best sited in isolation from surrounding foliage, if you have that option.

When fixing a box to the trunk of a tree, it should always be at such an angle that it leans slightly forwards, hole inclined slightly down. This not only avoids rain dropping or driving in, but also makes it that bit harder for a cat or squirrel to get at the hole.

A box fixed to a tree trunk is perhaps best sited so that branches do not project below or close above the box. In other words you ideally want a clear trunk, which gives birds an open view of the box and from it, with no branches to help predators reach it. If fixing your boxes up in winter, remember the difference that leaf cover will make in the summer. Siting the box well clear of branches not only suits the birds better, but it means that you as an observer will have an unobstructed view of the comings and goings of the birds. Half the pleasure of the nest box is lost if you cannot see it. If branches are too close to the box, saw them off.

The question as to what direction the entrance hole should face is a complicated one. Is it better facing north or east, or is there a difference anyway? Opinions differ, but east-facing seems popular with birds and people. Birds like a bit of sunshine to warm them up on a cold morning just as we do. Views on this differ greatly and in the end I prefer to ignore the arguments for compass directions and see it this way.

Consider which windows of your house overlook the proposed site. Which window will you look from most often? Perhaps the breakfast table and kitchen window. So site your box so that you can see it and its entrance hole. You might just find it more interesting to have the hole not facing your field of view directly but angled slightly to one side. This way, depending on the background, of course, you may catch more of the outline of the birds as they approach – a side view of them rather than a back view. So your most frequent viewpoint from the house (or perhaps the garden) towards that particular box will dictate the direction the box will face when you fix it. Forget the so-called preferred directions by birds. I've had boxes occupied facing all compass points. Don't forget there is a bird housing shortage – occupants of a free house don't complain about the view.

There is just one provision on the question of direction. If the box faces full south, it may get very hot for nestlings in a heat wave with the sun glaring full into the entrance hole. So maybe a south-facing box should have a larger roof overlap to keep the sun off, or tree branches higher up the trunk to provide shade. Perhaps, too, it should be of thicker wood for better insulation with maybe the odd extra breather hole in the base.

Do not fix a perch on or close to the nest box. The birds don't need it and squirrels and cats might find it helpful. Do not fix a nest box on the same post as a food tray or bird table, since birds cannot nest in peace if others are constantly coming near for food. Likewise do not hang nut feeders or coconuts or any food on a tree near to a nest box. Some bird tables sold in garden centres have a nest box built in to the bird table, e.g. in the roof area above a covered food table. They may look very pretty and it might seem a good idea, but it isn't. Birds do sometimes nest in these. A friend of mine has one such occupied every season by blue tits, but they must have a very troubled life, as most birds will protect their territory from others of the same species and constant battles will take place as the nesting pair tries to drive off other blue tits coming to feed. Such a situation can lead to birds deserting a nest.

A food table is also a magnet for predators such as squirrels and other vermin, who will just as soon eat eggs or young as scraps. If you have such a bird table combined with a nest box, seal up the entrance hole so it can't be used.

Don't buy or make a nest box with little windows or shutters or doors, made to look like a doll's house. These are unnatural and you are hoping to attract birds by imitating the natural. Don't site your nest box too close to a house window, however keen you are to get a good view. You'll only scare the birds off every time you pass by the window.

Some people like to believe they will encourage birds to build in a nest box by introducing a little nest material when the box is first fixed up – maybe a little moss or grass. I suppose the idea is to give the birds a hint as to what a nest box is for. I've never done this myself. If you feel like doing it, I suppose it can do no harm, provided you introduce only a small amount. Natural nest holes don't have this priming, and birds know all they need to know about how to build a nest without our help, so it seems unnecessary to me.

Most nest boxes have a hinged lid or removable lid. If yours has and you can't resist peeping inside occasionally, then try to do it with as little disturbance as possible to nesting birds. If you can, choose a time when you see the bird is off the nest. It may be hard to resist finding out when the first egg is laid, especially if you are new to bird gardening. This is understandable as it is very exciting when you become a bird parent for the first time. The birds find it exciting too and if you open a nest box lid and scare the sitting bird, she may find it so exciting she never comes back again! If possible, wait till you see the bird come off for feeding. After a while you get used to being a bird gardener. I never inspect my boxes as I am content to see the birds coming and going. You will soon know if a box is occupied without having to look inside.

Don't forget that a certain amount of prospecting for sites goes on, and often you might see a pair of blue tits in and out of a box for a day or two only to find great tits or nuthatches doing the same thing in the same box several days later. So the sight of a bird carrying nest material into a box does not necessarily indicate that it has set about serious nest building just yet. When they get down to serious building, you'll know it.

Some bird gardeners like to clear out old nests after the brood has flown or at the end of a season – box nesting birds will often rear two or even three broods in a season. They feel that it is best to remove what is by then dirty nest material, perhaps lice-infested, and maybe containing the odd infertile egg or even a dead nestling. Maybe they are right, but I don't do this myself. In nature an old nest would remain uncleared, unless the birds themselves cleared it up. Once my boxes are set up, I leave the birds well alone to get on with it. I'm sure the reason some bird gardeners get a low box occupancy rate is because they never leave it alone, constantly checking it and fiddling with it. Birds like privacy just as we do. Would you like living in your house if someone kept lifting the roof off to have a look in at you?

Despite all the hints and tips, some nest boxes still fail to attract occupants. Who knows why? There may be a reason none of us can identify. So if you run perhaps two seasons with a box in which no interest at all has been shown, why not try resiting it? It is obviously doing no good where it is.

The question of how deep the box is does matter. How much depth in inches is needed from the entrance hole to the base will depend on what birds are to occupy it, which we cannot predict in advance. It is likely to be a species from the list on page 47, and as we are going to average out our boxes to attract any or all of these, we'll make the hole-to-base depth so as to suit each of those species. I would think eight inches is about right, ten if you like. In nature birds would take pot luck anyway. If you buy your nest box, then you'll have to take what is given, but most nest box manufacturers do have some idea what they are doing. Some like to make the hole-to-floor height more like five inches, but if it is shallow, then there is always a danger that a cat or squirrel can scoop out nestlings. Don't worry about the youngsters scrambling out; they will when they're ready.

One point concerning depth is that the entrance hole should be positioned well up on the box front (or side if you prefer). The space between the hole and the roof is only waste anyway. So gain maximum safety depth for the contents by positioning your entrance hole well up.

There are all kinds of ways of fixing a nest box to a tree, some involving rubber washers or wooden spacers to keep the back of the box off the trunk, thus hoping to avoid rainwater soaking off the trunk through the box back. Go to these lengths if you wish but be prepared to modify your fixing methods according to the problems you face with a particular tree trunk, its shape, angle of tilt, bumps and branch stubs.

Some birds may use the nest box in winter for roosting. Put up your nest box any time you like, but late autumn is considered the best time as this gives the birds plenty of time to get used to them before spring.

If you are keen to photograph your birds, eggs or nestlings, then one possibility is to build a special box with a glass or transparent perspex sheet as a back and set the box against an aperture in, for instance, an outbuilding or garden shed. A second wooden 'back' will need to be made, which is fixed in place to cover the glass, and this is only removed during photography. You, as the photographer, can be installed inside the shed and out of sight of the birds, removing the second box back only after your camera and tripod are in place and then only for short spells. This sort of practice is best left to nature photographers, who are expert at it and can do it without putting the birds at risk. I've never done it myself, as I feel that for a novice there is too much risk of disturbing the birds. If you aim to try this, read a book about it first.

If inspecting the contents of your box, be particularly careful during the later days of fledging. If you frighten young birds who are not yet quite ready to leave the nest you may find them popping out like jack-in-the-boxes, and may have a terrible job trying to get them back in again. As fast as you put one back, another will jump out. I once had such an experience with young tawny owls, who kept leaping off a nest platform 30 feet up in a spruce tree, and it taught me a lesson I'll never forget, as young owls are not gentle with you.

Birds which readily take to enclosed nest boxes of the type described above are: blue tit, great tit, nuthatch, pied flycatcher, starling, house sparrow, tree sparrow.

Birds which sometimes will nest in this type of box but less readily than the above are: great spotted woodpecker, tree creeper, rock dove, collared dove, jackdaw, kestrel, coal tit and green woodpecker.

Some of these latter obviously need a much bigger box than discussed earlier.

If nuthatches take over your box, they will plaster a mud rim round the entrance hole till the hole is just the right size to suit them. Often, too, they will squeeze mud to cover any air gaps at the joints. This does not mean you are making your holes the wrong size – they just like to do it anyway!

Tree creepers like a narrow nest site with an opening or hole back and front and boxes are specially made to appeal to their unusual tastes. They are said to use this thin, tent-like type of nest box, but I've tried two or three over the years and not one of them was ever used, though we do have tree creepers nesting naturally.

Open-fronted nest boxes cater for birds which would in natural conditions nest in more open cracks, crevices, ledges, rock fissures and bankings. In concept the box is much like the enclosed type already described but has the upper half of the front completely open. Various sizes and patterns exist and are intended to adapt this type to the needs of its different users. Birds most likely to use this open-fronted box are: robin, blackbird, spotted flycatcher, wren, pied wagtail and occasionally thrushes. Some others might occasionally use such a box but really only by chance. The birds we are hoping to attract with them are confined to the above list. A suitable size for all these except the blackbird would be a floor area of four inches by four inches. A blackbird size should be about twelve inches by twelve inches floor area.

The birds which might use these open-fronted boxes are those seeking an open condition of nesting but one hidden from predators overhead and on all sides except the front. Such birds would in nature nest, for example, in ivy-clad walls, window ledges of outbuildings, cracks in masonry (rather than holes), wall-clinging greenery, and often in odd corners of old farmyards or industrial sites. Sometimes in nature these birds have a blind spot whereby the nest may be very obviously on view from a certain direction, yet quite concealed from others. All these species seem keen to be hidden from above in particular, where birds of prey might spot them. Some of these nesters are well known for occasionally selecting eccentric nesting sites – robins and wrens particularly may do this. So, in trying to attract them, we must offer them something which simulates their natural site preferences. Open-fronted boxes are only one way of doing this.

The number of birds who will take to this type of nesting box (and sometimes a nesting tray, as discussed later) are few in number relative to those taking an exclosed box. They include, however, some of our most endearing and confiding birds, birds of great personality and charm who will sometimes become, if not tame, then at least easy enough in our presence to regard our gardens as their rightful homes.

It seems to me that good luck and the idiosyncracy of the birds plays a larger part in the acceptance of this type of open-fronted box than with enclosed boxes. That these boxes are used there is no

Nuthatch at nestbox. *(Photo Paul Reinsch)*

Male Pied Flycatcher at nestbox. *(Photo Paul Reinsch)*

Pheasant taking bread. *(Photo author)*

Pair of Swallows at nest with young on purpose-made nesting shelf.
(Photo Paul Reinsch)

Long-tailed Tit at nest. *(Photo Paul Reinsch)*

Young House Martins peep out of nest under eaves. *(Photo Paul Reinsch)*

Dunnock attracted by bread. *(Photo Paul Reinsch)*

Jackdaw at birdtable. *(Photo Paul Reinsch)*

Wren feeding young in an old Swallow's nest. *(Photo author)*

A Grey Wagtail on its nest in an urn. *(Photo author)*

Moorhens – adult in foreground, as young of first brood feeds young of second brood. *(Photo Paul Reinsch)*

Adult Woodpecker feeding young at a nut feeder. *(Photo author)*

doubt, but the location may be almost as important as the box itself, and it is not unknown for birds of these species to be so contrary as to build a nest on the *roof* of such a box rather than inside it. Personally I've never found I've had a high success rate with these boxes. In my present home I don't use them at all, for the simple reason that we are troubled by grey squirrels, and by inviting birds to nest in such boxes I would simply be helping to provide an easy meal for the squirrels, who would most certainly find them.

In many gardens, however, these boxes can provide a good way of attracting nesting pairs of some of our favourite birds. In the smaller garden and backyard they may be especially effective, as they lend themselves well to hiding in corners where these species are prone to creeping and exploring. This group of birds includes a number, such as robins and wrens, whose approach to the nest may be frequently one of short stages rather than the more direct and open flight path of birds such as great tits who use enclosed boxes.

Open-fronted boxes can be sited at heights from about two feet upwards, except that at such a low level the boxes are vulnerable to cats or rats. If you are absolutely certain that no cats have access, then a range from two to six feet might suit. It might be safer to site them at heights above four feet up to perhaps seven or eight. The main consideration for these boxes is that they should blend in to some sort of cover, not so much in colour, but so as to be semi-concealed. A space where a stone is missing from a wall, tight against a wall where thick ivy grows around and perhaps partly over the box, a corner where tall plants half obscure it, a window sill of an outbuilding or garden shed, a suitable ledge or corner *inside* an outbuilding (as long as there is permanently open access): these are the kind of secret places such birds love to nest in.

For those inclined to make their own nest boxes, a triangular-shaped one is ideal for a corner position.

Simple nesting trays will be used by some birds – blackbirds, spotted flycatchers, occasionally song thrushes, chaffinches and even woodpigeons. These trays are merely nesting platforms with an edge piece to hold the nest in place. The bottom can be slatted rather than solid to let rain drain through. A degree of concealment is essential with these, as it is with open-fronted boxes. Sometimes unexpected species will take to trays or open-fronted boxes.

With the open-fronted nest box and the nesting tray, all you are really doing is providing an alternative for a bird which might naturally nest on e.g. a flat bough of a tree against an ivy-covered wall. So, just like a tree bough, it does not need to be a 'box' at all. A short shelf might be just as acceptable: a piece of waste timber perhaps three inches wide and an inch thick and of any length to suit the surroundings, say anywhere from one foot to one yard long. Fasten such a shelf five or six feet high with a couple of angle brackets against a wall or fence which has an ivy covering and you have a perfect nesting ledge for spotted flycatchers or half a dozen other shelf nesters. Put the shelf between the ivy and the wall. It might even be that such a shelf would wedge in tight without the need for brackets as strong ivy would hold it in place and would grip it ever tighter as it grew stronger.

6
Artificial Nesting Sites

WE HAVE ALREADY discussed nest boxes of varying types, but there are many ways of creating other artificial nesting places which garden birds might be induced to use. The same principle applies in making these nesting sites as applies with nest boxes, in so far as all the time the intention is to simulate nature, to offer suitable conditions, which today are becoming increasingly scarce in the wild, in order to provide birds with what they want but where we want it.

If we think back to our pond as an example, if you fill a hole with water, birds may drink and bathe in it but nothing will nest by it. Grow clumps of reeds on it as promontories and miniature islands and you have a chance.

A year or two ago I stuck a willow stick in my pond amongst a clump of reeds. When it sprouted, I cut back each twig to about six inches above water level. Next season a moorhen built its grassy nest intertwined amongst the cut-back twigs, which gave it a firmer support then the reeds would have done. As the willow sprouted, it gave extra leaf cover overhead. This same principle applies with the rest of our gardens.

Many birds nest in holes in masonry just as readily as in holes in trees. As property is maintained and masonry repointed, holes become increasingly scarce. Some years ago we repointed an out-building. A blue tit nested every year in an existing hole, so when repointing we left that hole untouched, and the birds continue to nest there every year. In that same building we removed an old galvanised pipe, which had once carried water, and left the hole deliberately unfilled. The very next season blue tits moved in and have nested there ever since.

On one end of the building, a sort of lean-to bit, some of the stones were missing and others were loose. A pied wagtail had once nested in a space where a stone had fallen out. In restoring that section, we left the space for the wagtail's nest, and one or two other missing stone holes were built round rather than filled in. The wagtail nested again in its old spot the following season, but then moved elsewhere later – wagtails are fickle nesters anyway and seem to like an occasional change of site. A song thrush built in one of the other gaps in the following season, though unfortunately squirrels took the eggs. So on just two walls of one building we were able to keep two existing nest sites, which continued in use, and we provided two new ones, which were used. The building described had no ivy growing on these walls, but an ivy covering would have greatly improved the prospects.

On another wall of that same building we planted some large-leaved ivy from a rooted stem taken from a friend's garden. Heaven knows what species it is, but it has massive leaves, some of them ten inches long, and looks as if it might be more at home in a South American jungle. It was not long before it reached first-storey height and had to be cut back each season. Its leaves offer wonderful cover and so far we have had blackbirds, pied wagtails, grey wagtails and hedge sparrows build nests in it, all less than six feet from the ground. The entire section of wall is only ten feet in length and the spread of ivy only six feet. One moral is that if you buy ivy, get the biggest-leaved variety you can. One year we had two nests in this ivy at the same time, though not of the same species, of course. That particular wall forms part of a quiet yard corner, which must help, but on the other hand the ivy is not twelve feet away from a much used con-servatory. The birds nesting there seem to more or less ignore people who are 'behind glass'.

This particular yard is only twelve feet square with walls on three sides. The ivy faces east. On the south-facing wall we planted a clematis, one of the Montana type which you don't cut back each year. After about five years the clematis had reached the wall top at about eight feet high. Blackbirds have nested in the clematis for two seasons now, despite the fact that on each occasion a pair of birds of another species had a nest at the same time in the ivy not twelve feet away on the adjacent wall.

As we restored an old stone wall in this same yard, we decided, just as ornament, to build a recess big enough to accept an urn to grow a trailing pot plant. One year a pair of pied wagtails nested in the actual urn, the nest resting inside the rim behind the plant. They reared a successful brood there even though we had to intrude occasionally to water the plant. The next year grey wagtails nested in the old pied wagtail nest in the urn! It seems urns are popular nest sites with some species. Of course, what made this site particularly attractive to the birds was that, being recessed, it was hidden from overhead predators.

On top of that a pair of blue tits nests in a hole in the third (plain) wall of that yard each season. So in a yard twelve feet square which is exceptionally close to a conservatory three pairs of birds nest every season. The only site fabrication we did was to provide the wall climbers, and, unintentionally, a nesting urn!

So, if restoring or rebuilding old walls, try to leave the odd hole or two to provide a more natural version of the open-fronted nest box. If building a new garden wall, you could probably plan to leave the old missing stone or brick here and there – even making some sort of random pattern of it. If you can plant some sort of wall-covering creeper on the wall, so much the better, as a hole in the wall with some frontal screen cover is doubly attractive. Of course, birds have a mind of their own and can be contrary. I left a stone out of an old dry stone wall in what I thought would be a perfect site for a robin. It's been there fifteen years now and I've never seen a bird even look at it!

Birds which nest in the lower height ranges are always short of nesting places: robins, wrens, hedge sparrows and sometimes pied wagtails. These will often nest as low as three feet, some of them lower. In most gardens there is a desperate shortage of places for them at these heights and they are often eager to use whatever you provide. I remember as a child wandering through fields of rhubard and finding nests of hedge sparrows in the rhubarb plants as there was simply no other cover.

As I write this, a pair of robins has a nest in a pile of logs I left lying after winter pruning. The log pile is only three feet high and three feet long and the logs are no longer than two feet each. I've watched the birds go in and out of this pile regularly. The cock stands guard nearby and when I approach, the hen flies out. Yet I cannot see any sign of the nest at all, so well hidden is it, even though I peer in on my hands and knees and I know the nest is there. This was an accidentally provided site. It just happens to be near an open area of lawn where very few robin sites are available to whichever pair of robins happens to have been pushed into this less nestable plot by other robins who have claimed the better territories. The neighbouring pair of robins has a nest on the ground on an uncultivated sloping bank of bluebells, underneath a grass tussock.

This is exactly the situation that pertains to many a town garden or new garden plot. It may not be practical to provide a pile of logs, but this example illustrates how keen such birds are to grab at anything resembling the kind of site they like.

The previous year, in almost the same part of the garden, my son was burning a pile of brushwood clippings which had been stacked there for only a few weeks, waiting for a chance to burn them on a fine day. They included evergreen branches such as Leylandii and spruce and the pile started off maybe eight feet high. He was removing a few branches at a time to the fire nearby when, at about the four-foot level, he came across a nest of young blackbird fledglings cheeping for food. He had to very quickly replace some of the top cover and leave the parents to get on with their job. That illustrates nicely how a solitary stand of cover in an otherwise open area seems to act as a special magnet, perhaps because the birds have ample view of approaching danger all round.

So for sites lacking this close-to-the-ground nesting cover, the occupation rate can be very high if you make some attempt to provide something suitable. A bundle of old twigs and small branches, a windfall or perhaps prunings that never got burned, can be tied together in the middle with string. The longest sticks need to be about four feet high with plenty of gnarled bits in the middle. An odd cutting or two from an evergreen such as cypress or holly helps, as even when the leaves die there is still some cover. Tie in a few bracken strands or rose prunings and make it tight in the middle with ends sticking outwards top and bottom, wigwam-like. Wedge or tie such a bundle firmly into an odd wall corner. For good measure scatter a few handfuls of fallen leaves over it when next clearing up, or a few grass cuttings. This may provide an ideal site for a robin, wren or hedge sparrow, which might nest in it or between the wigwam and the wall it wedges against.

You could provide several such wigwams depending on what space you have. If you can site one where grass or nettles will grow up, into and around it, so much the better. A clump of nettles can be put to work for you in this way by setting a wigwam amongst them before growth starts. Nettles grow early in the season — mine are a foot high in mid-April – and they will help keep predators away. In a neat garden then, you would obviously site these in a less conspicuous part. Most gardens have unsightly bits somewhere, so put these areas to good use.

Certain trees are amazing survivors – willow, for instance. You can cut almost any stick from willow (it does not matter which type), push it into soil, and it will start to sprout. If you have willow trees, they will tend to grow rapidly and need constant lopping or pruning. Any bit of willow cutting will do – they even grow if you happen to stick them in soil *upside down*. This is best done in autumn or winter, but they usually grow whenever you do it, though they may die back a bit at first. I sometimes make a frame of three or four such sticks each about four feet high, pushed into the soil and linked together with a bit of string or wire, like the box frame of a tent.

Plant a clump of nettles in the middle if you have some you've weeded out from the cultivated areas. Then plant up to half a dozen blackberry roots round your frame. You don't have to buy cultivated ones as wild brambles will do just as well. If you already have cultivated ones elsewhere in the garden, heel a tip into the ground and in a few weeks you will have another rooted plant, which can be cut free, dug out and planted round your frame.

Train your blackberries round the willow framework. The willow will sprout and can be clipped like a small bush till the blackberries grow into a thick tangle. A few evergreen stems can be pushed into the middle until the growth thickens up. This tangled tent will make possible nest sites for undergrowth birds and, if nothing nests in it, at least blackbirds and thrushes will eat the berries in the autumn.

You can clip and prune your evergreens to make them more likely possibilities as nest sites. Once you get higher than about ten feet in evergreens such as cypress or spruce, the number of birds which may nest in them above that height are few – maybe woodpigeons and tawny owls – but your appeal is to few species. The same applies to larch. Any smaller birds nesting above that height (certain finches, for instance) will just as soon nest lower if you give them no other choice. Clipping the tops off spruce will gain you little, as the base parts seen to sprout little differently for it. With cypress, however, top pruning does force denser growth lower down, and bear in mind that if it gets higher than fifteen feet, you're going to have a terrible job if you do later decide to try to lop it shorter. It might be as well, therefore, especially, in a smaller garden, to keep cypress fairly low-cut – eight feet high is plenty. You gain light and lose little in the way of nest sites. Despite their strong growth, cypress are prone to blowing over in a gale and keeping them cut low removes a lot of the wind hazard. Pruning to restrict the height of cypress is fine, but don't try to prune too narrowly or you'll end up with just trunks and a few dead branch stubs sticking out. Leave plenty of thickness in the hedge for healthy growth and good bird cover.

If you have odd clumps of brambles or gorse growing in a tangled mass amongst rank grasses, try raising them off the ground a couple of feet by wedging forked sticks amongst them. Small clusters of raised brambles or gorse are fine as sites for several species, but don't let the clumps spread too far afield or too low to the ground. The principle of small clumps of dense vegetation amongst open spaces always applies.

Train brambles or climbers such as wild honeysuckle, clematis or climbing roses round an old field post or big fence post and the flat top will provide a possible site, as long as some leafy cover runs over it. A clump or two of bracken is useful in some unused corner but don't let it get out of hand or it will take over.

Birds will often need help in finding nesting materials. A string or net bag, such as an old onion bag, can be used to contain raked-up leaves, sheeps' wool, grass strands, dog hairs, and any bits of soft materials. Hang such a bag on to a wall or fence, preferably where you can get the benefit of having it on view, and birds will soon find it and make use of its contents in nest building. This applies especially in town gardens where birds may have less choice of naturally available materials than in the country.

Robins will sometimes nest in old kettles. If you have an old kettle and you want to try this, wedge the kettle tightly into a wall or low bush, spout down as a drainer, open top to the front. Old paint cans will sometimes be used in this way, but make sure the can leans slightly forward or it will fill with water during rain. Better still, punch a few drain holes in its, just in case. I'm not one for kettles personally as I think I can make something as effective and less unsightly, but if you like the look of a kettle in your garden, good luck with it. As it happens, my Robins are contrary and like to nest in low trees or bushes, which is not traditional for robins, but birds are individuals and it may be that mine have learned they are safer from squirrels in a thick bush than in a ledge type of site.

If you have a barn or outbuilding, you can try to encourage owls. Barn owls are principally the ones that might come into such a build-ing, provided you have some sort of high opening or skylight. You can build a platform for them just inside such an entrance hole, a platform with an open box area maybe a foot square and a rim three inches high or so, to prevent eggs or nestlings rolling out. Something like an old tomato box would do, if strong enough. I tried this only once and owls did come into my barn, which was used as a garage at the time, though they didn't nest there. Instead they would bring in the night's catch to eat it on the rafters. As my car used to be parked below, I would be greeted in the morning with a blood-splattered roof and uneaten bits of dead rat lying where they had fallen!

A friend nearby had an owl fall down the chimney one night into the living room where it made a terrible mess, spreading soot every-where. If you plan to encourage owls, put a mesh grid over your chimney and buy a red car.

Outbuildings can also attract swallows, which are beautiful birds, but messy. They will, if they like the look of it, readily nest in any convenient outbuilding or under a lean-to type of garage roof or carport. They prefer to nest on a rafter close to the roof rather than attempt to stick their mud nests directly to the wall/roof joint itself.

Nailing to the wall a batten of timber maybe three inches thick at such a height that its top is about six inches below roof level may help, just to give them something to build on. You must be sure they have a permanently open access, as if someone closes a door by mistake, disaster will follow. Swallows will carry their nestlings' waste out before dropping it in flight at any distance over ten yards or so. If that's where you park your car, then you know what to expect.

For the first hour or so after daybreak birds seem less wary of human presence than later in the day. So occasionally an unusually early start to the day can be a rewarding experience for a bird gardener. Once full daylight arrives, birds soon busy themselves with feeding, and again the early riser will find the bird table a more interesting place at that time – my woodpeckers attend my bird table regularly in the early morning, whilst they are far less keen to come down later in the day.

Nest building for most garden birds takes place in April and early May. Nesting birds have certain peak periods of activity in their working day. Many birds seem to concentrate on nest building for an hour or so in the morning, though not in the first hour of daylight. At this time of year an hour or so between 8am and 10am is often nest building time. They seem to have a second building session in the early evening, roughly between 6pm and 8pm. In between there can be long periods of apparent inactivity as the birds wander about seemingly at random without regard to the place they are building, and during this time they can be less interesting to observe. The same time schedule does not apply for all species nor even for all pairs of birds within a particular species. You will only find out by watching for yourself, but if you can establish the pattern of your own garden birds, that may mean you can concentrate your birdwatching time in the most effective periods.

The nesting season is the most exciting time in the bird gardener's year. It is the time when the results of your efforts can be seen to pay off or otherwise. As I write this in the first week of May, most resident garden birds have eggs or young. As I checked round my garden this morning I came across the following nests: a grey wagtail sitting on six eggs, a pied wagtail on five, a robin on four, a hedge sparrow on two, a chaffinch on four, a woodpigeon on two, a moorhen on four, several nests each of blackbirds and song thrushes with eggs, and long-tailed tits feeding uncounted young (they seem particularly early this year). High in the cypress trees we have nesting goldfinches, greenfinches, more woodpigeons, more chaffinches and goldcrests, but to find their nests involves searching with ladders, which I am not inclined to do, as I am content to know they are there.

Of my enclosed nest boxes, three are occupied by great tits and four more by blue tits, whilst two more pairs of blue tits have nests in holes in walls. One pair each of nuthatches and pied flycatchers are occupying enclosed boxes, the latter just building. A pair of swallows is just building in an outbuilding and a pair of wrens has just completed a nest. Almost all of these nests are within twenty yards of the house. Additionally a pair of pheasants has a nest in long grass under a Scots pine, a pair of blackcaps is just building in some bushes, a pair of dippers is nesting by the stream which passes my garden and a pair of coal tits and a pair of tree creepers are nesting somewhere in my boundary trees, though I have not found the nests. There are also other nesting pairs of some of these species, whose nests I have not stumbled across.

With the exception of the enclosed nest box users, all these birds are occupying natural sites but sites that I have created by planting the right kind of trees and climbers in the right sorts of places. None of these were nesting here when we took the house, at which time our nesting population was limited to a pair or two of blackbirds and thrushes. And the nesting season is just getting into full swing!

Making a Hide

I have watched birds since I was a youngster of seven or eight and have always found a certain magic about them, especially in the nesting season. And whilst the practice of making a hide has long been known, I had never bothered to take the trouble, as I was not particularly interested in taking photographs. This year, however, a friend of mine insisted on making one and bringing it over to my garden to try it out. We set it up in the third week of May within view of a bullfinch's nest with young. We set the hide itself on top of some sectional scaffolding so that we stood inside the hide at about eight feet from the ground. A wooden plywood floor topped the scaffolding. The whole assembly must have taken no more than ten minutes to erect.

Within three days the hide was moved closer to the nest, finally to about four feet distant. The birds completely ignored it and continued feeding unaware of an observer in the hide. To see these beautiful birds at such close quarters was an experience I shall never forget. I could have reached out my arm to touch them. The colours of the plumage were even more striking in reality than in brightly-painted illustrations in books. It was a magical experience.

So for all those who, like myself, have always regarded the whole business of making a hide as too much of a fag, I can only say you just don't know what you are missing. Our hide was made from an old tent re-sewn into an upright rectangular structure with four brush handles for corner-posts and looked something like a camping toilet. It served the purpose, but now we know all about design faults in hide-making. If you plan to make yourself one, and it really is well worth the effort, here are a few pointers. Make it high enough to be able to stand upright inside it – standing in a hunched position is no joke. Make it wide enough to be able to get a small folding camp stool inside. Make a number of camera lens' holes in the front to give you a choice of camera heights, and give each hole a cover you can drop on the inside when not using that particular observation hole. Provide some ventilation holes to let air circulate as it gets very hot in the sun. Consider some sort of sloping or pitched roof – our roof filled with water during rain to form a small pond which trickled down onto the occupants for hours.

If working at any height from the ground, anchor things down for safety. In a breeze our hide on scaffolding swayed like a top-heavy ship in a swell – ultimately one corner post slid out of place and the hide collapsed about my ears. You feel particularly helpless acting as a human tentpole eight feet from the ground and can quite lose your attention on focussing.

7
Birds in Your Garden

Blackbird *(Turdus merula)*
One of our best-known resident birds and a visitor to virtually every garden. It is principally a ground feeder, searching lawns and vegetable plots for worms and insects and also foraging in hedge bottoms, where it will turn over leaves to reveal hidden creatures. In autumn it will eat all kinds of berries and fruits. It will come to bird tables but principally in hard winter weather, and even then is happier feeding on fallen titbits on the ground. In winter it will eat all manner of household scraps, particularly fats and cheeses but also fruit peelings and sultanas. In summer the birds find plenty of insects and will probably not bother to take food put out for them, though in a small town garden with less foraging space they might.

Blackbirds are amongst the earliest garden birds to nest, sometimes building as early as March and often having eggs by the first week of April. As early nesters, they will frequently go for evergreens or sometimes a leaf-carrying beech hedge, as there is little cover in March. Cypress are favourites for first nests of the season.

They are renowned for nesting in eccentric places, using any convenient ledge or shelf where they feel there is adequate cover: a shelf in an outbuilding, on top of lumber in a shed, a tread on a set of stepladders, a bumper on a railway engine. Every year blackbirds are in the local press for their unusual nesting places. It is this leaning towards the eccentric which gives us the opportunity of fabricating nest sites to attract them. They will take to open-fronted nest boxes with a base about twelve inches square, or sometimes open nest trays if set against a wall corner where there might be some overhead cover such as a shrub or wall creeper. Personally I've never had success with blackbirds in open-fronted boxes, though a pair once built on top of one in preference to inside it! If you are short of early nest cover, then a bundle of sticks tied together and packed with grasses and bracken and fixed in a quiet corner might just work. Several pairs in my garden nest almost exclusively in cypress trees and hawthorn hedges, with a pair or two in spruce.

The nest is very like that of a song thrush but the mud lining is itself lined with leaves and grass. The nest is commonly between six and eight feet from the ground, though with eccentric sites it could be higher. The four or five eggs have a pale blue-green ground with brown spots and freckles. Incubation takes roughly two weeks, and the same for fledging. Several broods may be reared in a season.

Occasionally blackbirds will have a few white feathers, as they are more prone than most species to have an albino streak. When this happens, it means you can recognise an individual from others, which makes following its activities more interesting.

Blue Tit *(Parus caeruleus)*
Common resident bird and well known in every garden. They are busy, inquisitive birds and will readily take food from a bird table, including peanuts, seeds, fatty foods such as suet, and meat bones. They also eat many insects including greenfly and caterpillars.

They take readily to enclosed nest boxes and can squeeze into an entrance hole only one inch in diameter, though I use 1¼ inches myself. Great tits, being a larger and more dominant bird, may take over the choice nest boxes if a 1¼-inch hole is used, but a solution to this problem is simply to put up more boxes so that there is ample accommodation for both. This year I added ten new boxes to my garden with the smaller size of hole and due to unforeseen circumstances they were not erected until the first week of April, which is unduly late. By the middle of May four of the ten were occupied by sitting blue tits, which may be some measure of the shortage for this species, and the degree to which larger birds dominate the bigger boxes.

Blue tits will also nest in holes and cracks in walls, where they tend to have the advantage over larger hole nesters. The nest is built of moss, wool and feathers in April. The eggs number from seven to ten, sometimes more, and are white with light red spots. Incubation takes two weeks, fledging two to three weeks. One brood is normal. The birds soon become accustomed to the presence of humans and tend to go about their business without much regard to passing people. They are not averse to pecking through milk bottle tops for a drink and our daily milk delivery has to be permanently covered to stop this.

These birds sometimes get a fixation for pecking on glass windows and when they do, it is very difficult to stop them. For some weeks one took to tapping on our landing window at first light, about 4am, which is a little sooner than I would waken by choice. This was finally stopped only by tying some netting round that particular window till it grew out of the habit. The reasons for this action are hard to determine, as it was certainly not a matter of picking out spiders from window corners. On another occasion one took it into its head to attack the glass wing mirror of my car, perching on the sill and flying at it aggressively for some good few minutes each day for several days. It was this that convinced me that the reason was that the bird saw in its own reflection what it took to be a rival bird in its territory. Other species sometimes do this too (chaffinches, for instance), but blue tits seem more prone to do it than others.

Bullfinch *(Pyrrhula pyrrhula)*
Resident bird of somewhat retiring nature. It is notorious for its habit of eating buds from fruit trees and it is perhape unfortunate that it is at its most conspicuous when seen in the open doing this. Its overall stocky appearance with heavy bill, black cap and red underparts (pink in the female) is unmistakable. For the most part, however, the bullfinch spends its time under the cover of foliage in woods and copses, hedgerows and thicket, parks and gardens, so that it is seldom seen clearly, if at all. Its secretive nature gives the impression of it being a rarer bird than is the case.

Bullfinches feed mainly on the seeds of weeds and on berries, as well as on fruit tree buds. I had often noticed them with mixed feelings on my garden fruit trees in spring, but did not realise they nested in my garden till I found the nest this year with determined searching. The hen sits very tight, often refusing to leave the nest till one is within inches. The nest is built in late April or May, and consists of a very thinly built platform of sticks, not unlike a smaller version of a woodpigeon's nest. Within this platform is the nest proper, made of grasses, moss and fine roots (often black roots). The nest is very well hidden in an evergreen or dense hedge and usually out of reach at eight or ten feet.

They are said to eat peanuts and seeds from a hopper, but I've never seen mine do this, so presumably they find adequate natural food. The presence of fruit trees may well attract them to your garden as well as dense nesting cover. Mine nest in cypress, the all-purpose nesting tree. Bear in mind that a ten-foot-high nest with overhead cover will mean you need to have your nesting trees at least twelve feet tall.

The four or five eggs are laid in early May and have a blue-green ground with spots and streaks of dark brown or purple, especially at the larger end. If you come across a nest, it is possible you may not see the birds for some time, but no other finch makes this sort of loose twiggy platform of a nest, so you cannot mistake it. Incubation takes just under two weeks, fledging about the same. The cock will bring food to the hen at the nest and the young are fed by regurgitation by both parents. Two broods or more are reared each season.

Chaffinch *(Fringilla coelebs)*

One of our commonest resident birds and recognised by everyone. It haunts gardens and orchards, parkland and hedgerows. It often becomes very tame and soon learns to come down for crumbs to picnicking visitors at countryside beauty spots or motorway laybys, and, of course, in gardens too. The chaffinch feeds mostly on seeds and will come to a bird table seed hopper for all kinds of seeds and also food scraps of a very varied nature. Chaffinches love peanuts and will struggle to cling on to nut feeder grills and even attempt to hover very briefly and awkwardly whilst extracting nuts. They are not very good at hovering but they try determinedly and are amusing to watch. They also consume a good proportion of insects and, when not at a bird table, are mainly ground feeders.

The nest is a very beautiful affair, small and neat with a deep cup, often placed in a fork of a tree close to the main trunk, where the mossy colour blends well with that of the tree bark. It is made of grass and fine roots and often has much moss and lichen about its exterior, the interior being lined with feathers. Sometimes bits of coloured wool or other decorative materials are incorporated. It is easy to overlook such a nest in, for instance, an apple tree, as it can blend in so well, especially on a lichen-covered trunk. At other times it will nest in a hedgerow or a conifer such as cypress, in a climbing rose against a wall or on a rose pergola. It will nest in shrubbery but usually the outer areas, where it is more open and lighter, and not in a dark or gloomy place. Chaffinches will sometimes use a nesting tray if set in one of these places where a little greenery will grow over and around it, but it is not a bird often associated with boxes or trays.

The nest is usually at a height of more than five feet and less than eight. In our own garden, early nests have often been in cypress or spruce, which are some of the few sites offering cover as early as April. At other times they have nested in climbing roses. Building takes place in April, eggs being laid late in April or early May, usually four or five in number. The ground colour varies but is usually light brown (sometimes light green) and spotted with red-brown and black dots and streaks. Chaffinch eggs vary more than those of many garden birds and so are always interesting to see. Often the marks will be clustered in a zone or circle around the larger end, sometimes on the whole clutch, but more often a single egg will show this variation. Once seen, chaffinch eggs cannot be forgotten, and whilst the nest is similar to a goldfinch's, the eggs are quite different and cannot be mistaken. Incubation takes two weeks, fledging about the same. Two broods are often reared in a season.

Coal Tit *(Parus ater)*

A resident bird frequenting gardens, copses and woods, particularly, it is said, conifers. The white patch on the back of its neck distinguishes it at once. This bird feeds on insects and seeds but will attend the bird table for the same sort of foods as other titmice – fats, peanuts and suet, particularly in harder winter weather. Coal tits feed on my peanut hopper all year round, though they are far less numerous than blue or great tits, and will always give way to these other, more aggressive birds in the pecking order.

Coal tits nest in a hole in a wall or a tree, sometimes a hole in a bank. They nest nearer to the ground than blue tits or great tits, sometimes in the ground itself, and will also take to eccentric places such as flowerpots, gratings, letterboxes etc, and, of course, enclosed nest boxes. Nest box size should be the same as for blue tits. It seems to me that these birds are less likely to occupy a nest box than blue or great tits. We have two or three pairs of coal tits in our garden all year round but only one pair nests in a nest box, even though quite a number are placed low, and this particular box is eight feet up!

The nest is built of moss, hairs and feathers and the seven to eleven (sometimes more) white eggs with red spots are laid in late April or early May. Incubation takes 2½ weeks, fledging just over two weeeks. One brood is normal, but occasionally they are double-brooded.

Coal tits will come to your garden along with blue tits and for the same kind of food, principally nuts.

Collared Dove *(Streptopelia decaocto)*

Now a widespread resident bird, yet only really entered this country as a breeding bird in the 1950s. It is a pretty dove, relatively tame, and soon settles in to visit gardens for food. It feeds on much the same sort of food as the woodpigeon and will eat anything from household scraps to peas and beans, fruit and grain.

The nest is a thin platform and the two white eggs are laid from April onwards, as several broods may be reared in the long season. Incubation takes 2½ weeks; fledging the same.

This is an endearing bird and often encouraged in gardens and parks, which may account for its phenomenally rapid spread. It seems to take to town and city gardens where it is often commoner than in the countryside. In my own garden I have never seen one, yet there are some in the village not a quarter of a mile away.

Goldfinch *(Carduelis carduelis)*

Perhaps our most beautiful finch. It does visit gardens as well as more open country, parkland and wasteland, but if you have a well-kept and tidy garden, you may never see one in it. The goldfinch eats seeds of many kinds but especially seeds of thistles and dandelions and of many other plants we commonly regard as weeds. So if you are a tidy gardener and quick with the weed-killer, they are unlikely to linger in your garden. In my garden there is no shortage of goldfinch food in the form of weeds, and the birds are about all year round. They are especially noticeable in winter when small family groups of them will visit clumps of seeded weeds. In spring, when they break into pairs, they are often less in evidence and they are said to change their diets more towards insects at that time, and are even more secretive when nesting.

If you cannot bear the thought of allowing weeds to grow rampant in the hope of attracting goldfinches, then perhaps you should buy one or two giant thistle plants or teasels from your garden centre and set them in a conspicuous place so that they can be seen to be intentional rather than weeds you have missed. Goldfinches will also feed in larch trees in spring.

They are said to visit bird tables for seeds in a seed hopper, but I've no experience of this, as in my garden they can find all the seeds they want naturally and I don't buy seeds for any of my resident birds. They will take peanuts, though mine never do.

The nest is a very neat and beautiful one not unlike that of a chaffinch and is made of moss and grasses, fine roots and hairs, and supposedly thistledown. They often nest higher than the chaffinch, perhaps even twenty or thirty feet up, and do not nest until the leaf cover is well out, usually in mid-May. For these reasons the nest is more likely to go unnoticed than that of the chaffinch. They are said to like to nest in orchards.

If you find the nest with eggs, you cannot mistake them for chaffinch eggs, being five or six in number and of a pale green or blue-white ground with red and dark red spots and smaller in size than those of the chaffinch. Incubation lasts two weeks; so does fledging.

Once you've had goldfinches in your garden, you'll want them back again. If you can't bear the thought of weeds, buy finch seed and offer it in a hopper in winter and spring.

Great Spotted Woodpecker *(Dendrocopus major)*

A resident woodland bird and will spend most of its time there hunting for insects and grubs, often high in the branches of mature trees. It also eats certain conifer seeds. It will visit parkland and orchards and gardens. It is very fond of peanuts and also suet, fats and marrow-bones hung from a string. When eating peanuts in a mesh feeder, it can be heard tapping quite noisily from 20 or 30 yards away.

It is a shy and nervous bird and seldom noticed except when at a bird table, where it is usually a timid feeder and will fly off with its strange undulating flight at the slightest excuse. Its presence in the vicinity is often advertised by the echo of its drumming or knocking sound, which is not, as might be imagined, the noise of it drilling in wood, but a territorial 'song' produced by rapping its beak rapidly on wood, a sound which can vary quite a bit according to the tree size. It often drums in the early morning.

The great spotted woodpecker excavates a nest hole in a tree, often high up at twenty or 30 feet. It is said to take to nest boxes of the enclosed type with a two-inch hole, base size of six inches square and hole-to-base height of fifteen inches. They may use the same hole or nest box each year. Nest boxes need positioning higher than twelve feet, ideally twenty.

A pair nests every year in a clump of beech woods close to us but they have never nested in my garden. They do come down to feed on peanuts every day, however, and bring the young with them in season. They fly off as soon as they catch sight of us through the window, and yet a friend of mine nearby has birds that totally ignore occupants of his house from a bird table at a similar distance from the window.

The four to six glossy white eggs are laid in late May or June and take two weeks to hatch. Fledging takes a further three weeks and one brood is usual. This is the likeliest of the woodpeckers to visit your garden.

Great Tit *(Parus major)*

A resident bird found in the majority of gardens as well as woods, copses and parks. This is a bird which eats a great variety of food and responds well to encouragement. It will take what it wants from all kind of household scraps but is especially fond of peanuts and coconuts; seeds, especially sunflower seeds; and fatty foods such as suet and bacon rind; and also eats insects such as caterpillars and spiders.

A constant supply of food will help ensure that great tits live in and around your garden. Once you have the birds feeding with you, it is a short step to getting them to accept a nest box, as they will very willingly take to enclosed boxes with a 1¼-inch diameter hole, floor size of five inches by five inches, and hole height from floor of eight inches; but a box with larger dimensions will also be used, when the birds will introduce more nest material. Too big an entrance hole, however, will let in house sparrows or starlings if you have them around.

They may investigate nest boxes as possible sites as early as March, and, of course, may well roost in them throughout the winter. Nesting proper begins in April and the nest of grass, moss, leaves, fur, feathers or anything soft will have a full clutch of between six and eight eggs (sometimes more) by the end of April or early May. The eggs are white with red spots.

Great tits seem happy to accept a nest box even quite close to a house. One of ours is not six feet from a house window and the birds soon get used to people moving about behind glass and seem to pretty well ignore us. Height is not a very important factor, so position your box(es) between about five feet and seven feet high, so that you can reach them and observe them conveniently. Incubation lasts two weeks and the male will feed the sitting hen with an occasional tempting caterpillar, which is interesting to watch.

Fledging takes about three weeks. Great tits will use the same nest box or site year after year. Occasionally they will nest in an eccentric place such as an upturned flowerpot or a letterbox, which only goes to illustrate the shortage of nest holes and their keenness to take to nest boxes when offered the chance. One brood is normal but second broods do occur.

Greenfinch *(Carduelis chloris)*
A common resident bird of stocky proportions which readily visits gardens where it will breed if conditions appeal. Green linnet was a name sometimes used in the past. Like many finches, it feeds mainly on seeds, berries and grains. It can be attracted to a bird table very easily by offering seeds in a hopper or peanuts of which it is especially fond.

These birds haunt parkland, shrubberies, hedgerows and gardens. The nest is usually in a thick hedgerow or a dense cluster of shrubbery and is placed above six feet high, often closer to ten. Sometimes a number of pairs will nest within close proximity, like a small, scattered colony.

The nest is built of twigs, moss, roots and grasses, lined with finer materials and feathers. It is less skilfully built than that of the chaffinch, being more loosely woven. The four to six eggs are laid in late April or early May. They are slightly larger than chaffinch eggs, having a pale green or pale blue ground with spots and blotches of red-brown and black. Incubation takes roughly two weeks, fledging two weeks also. Two broods may be reared in a season, occasionally three.

The greenfinch will not take artificial nest sites but can be encouraged by feeding nuts and seeds. If you cultivate a good dense hedge including some taller hawthorns or cypress trees, it may well nest with you.

Green Woodpecker *(Picus viridis)*

A bird more often heard than seen. It is a resident bird living in old woods and parkland or more open country with old deciduous trees, where it seeks insect larvae in the branches and dark fissures, using its long, flexible tongue to extract them from crevices. Its presence is often announced by its call, which is reminiscent of a maniacal laugh -kew,kew,kew, kew,kew. This call carries over long distances, especially if echoing through woodland, and is sometimes uttered during its oddly undulating flight. The bird is said to visit bird tables for suet and fats, but whilst we have green woodpeckers within a quarter of a mile of our garden, I've never seen one at my bird table. We hear their calls frequently and sometimes see the birds fly past, but they seem to have no inclination to visit my garden, which may be on account of the lack of ancient trees.

It is doubtful whether you can attract green woodpeckers by putting out food, though suet or a marrowbone might be worth trying. The birds excavate their own nest hole in a decaying tree, so a natural attraction would be aged and rotting trees, which few gardens can provide. They will sometimes take to nest boxes of the enclosed type, and you could try an oversize one with a base six inches square and an entrance hole 2½-inches in diameter. A few wood shavings or a little sawdust inside might give it more appeal. In nature the green woodpecker excavates a deep nest hole, so your hole-to-floor height needs to be at least twelve inches and is better at fifteen. A height in excess of fifteen feet probably stands a better chance than a low box. The problem is that this kind of box may appeal to starlings, which are more aggressive birds and will take over.

The five to seven glossy, white eggs are laid in May, or perhaps late April. Incubation takes 2½ weeks, fledging about the same time. One brood is normal.

Grey Wagtail *(Motacilla cinerea)*

A resident bird, less common than the pied and more common in hilly northern districts. It is a bird that lives not far from water, especially shallow, flowing water rather than lakes. It does visit farmyards and country gardens but is unlikely to nest unless suitable sites are present near to water. The preferred nesting site is somewhat similar to that of the pied wagtail – a rocky crevice, a hole in a bank or wall, amongst steep rocks etc., sometimes quite close to running water.

The nest is like the pied wagtail's. The eggs are laid in late April or May, four to six in number. They have a dirty, creamy white ground tinged with a dull shade of light brown. Incubation and fledging take about two weeks each, as with the pied.

There is nothing you can do to encourage this bird other than providing a stream or shallow pond and similar nesting sites to the pied, and cross your fingers. They come to my garden but it's probably only the running water that attracts them. This year my pair has taken over and renovated a two-year-old pied wagtail's nest inside a flower urn on a window sill. The nest is about 50 yards from water, so they don't have to have a waterside home, by any means.

Hedge Sparrow *(Prunella modularis)*

It is difficult for even the beginner to fail to recognise the hedge sparrow. Everyone knows the bird by this name, despite attempts by naturalists for the last 50 years to insist on calling it by the older name of dunnock, or the never popular hedge accentor or even hedge warbler, the argument being that this bird is not related to the less popular house sparrow.

The hedge sparrow is mostly a bird of low thickets and hedges, undergrowth and the ground, where it largely feeds. It will sometimes feed on a bird table but is far more inclined to search for titbits that drop from it while other birds are feeding. It will eat small crumbs of almost anything cooked when so inclined, and certain seeds, as well as crumbs dropping from a peanut feeder. It is a bird that gets on quietly with its own business, not so much being shy as keeping itself within the kind of feeding area it prefers.

One particular bird waits for me at the same spot every morning when I feed my chickens, till I throw it a few pellets of chicken food (even though these seem on the large side for it). This bird and others will readily visit the chicken feed trough to pick out choice bits of meal at any time of day.

The male and female look exactly alike. The nest is usually placed low down, less than four feet and often between two and three feet from the ground. It will nest in thick hedges such as hawthorn or beech. Early in the season it goes for evergreens such as holly or gorse or clipped Cupressus. The nest is of small twigs, grass and moss. The four to six sky blue eggs are laid from late April and take twelve days to hatch, twelve more before the young leave the nest. Two broods will be reared, sometimes three.

The hedge sparrow will not take artificial sites but will nest willingly in gardens where the right sort of low and dense shrubby cover exists. It will sometimes nest in ivy or other wall creepers, and in the absence of the right sort of hedge may well nest in bundles of sticks and twigs tied together and fixed in a quiet corner, especially if tall grasses grow in and around the twigs.

These birds will stay in the garden all year round, especially if there is a constant supply of food to help when they may have difficulty finding their own, e.g. in snow. Males will strongly defend a territory in the nesting season.

House Martin *(Delichon urbica)*

Arrives back in its summer haunts in April. Originally this bird would have nested on cliffs but today it uses mainly buildings as its nest sites and usually returns year after year to the same site. Like the swallow, it spends most of its time on the wing feeding on insects and cannot be attracted to the garden by any sort of food you can provide. It often feeds over water where insects gather.

House martins nest in small colonies, the size depending to a large extent on the site. They nest mainly under the overhanging eaves of houses and porches and presumably overcrowding on some sites forces some birds to prospect for new ones. A friend of mine built a new house a few years ago and within two years had a colony of half a dozen pairs nesting under his verandah, which is only at first-floor level but has a wide overhang. The birds must have found this an ideal site, as they simply arrived and took up residence.

Like swallows, house martins build their nests of mud which is gathered from ponds or puddles. The cup is more complete than that of the swallow, and is lined with feathers. The pure white eggs usually number four or five and are laid from about late May or June, taking two weeks to incubate. The young take three weeks to fledge. Two broods, or even three, may be reared.

Artificial nests can be bought today and fixed in suitable places under house eaves. Even if these nests are not used themselves, they may well encourage birds to see the site as a colony home and begin to build their own nests as part of it. You may need to fix up two or three, if your artificial nests are to do the trick. Under the lintel of a bedroom window can be a good place, as you then have the added advantage of being able to see the birds coming and going as you awaken.

Like swallows, house martins can be messy. A plank fixed on angle brackets on the wall below the nests may help, but is probably only a partial solution. If you think you will mind the mess, don't encourage them. If you have martins already established, then you're probably used to it by now anyway.

Jackdaw *(Corvus monedula)*

Bold, even cheeky birds, resident and common everywhere. They are also notorious egg thieves and will eat nestlings too, so that most bird gardeners may be keen to repel them rather than attract them. They frequent buildings, especially ruins where many nest holes may abound, but also woodland where they nest in holes in trees. In buildings they will often nest in colonies, but in a woodland situation suitable sites more often occur singly and then colony nesting is not possible.

They will come to a bird table or ground feeding trough, often when not welcome, and will eat any household scraps as well as corn and cereals and berries. They come to my garden feeder in winter especially, which I don't particularly mind, but in the nesting season their occasional presence is less welcome, as they are just as likely to empty any nests seen in passing. In feeding, they will occasionally keep company with crows or rooks but, being smaller and more agile, the jackdaws usually get in and out first.

They will sometimes take to enclosed nest boxes if an oversized model is made to suit their needs. This involves a six-inch diameter entrance hole and a box with a floor area eight inches square and hole-to-floor distance to eight inches.

The nest is a pile of sticks with a lining of grass, wool or hair. The four to six eggs are greenish-blue spotted and splashed with brown and grey or black. They are laid in April or early May. Incubation takes 2½ weeks, fledging four to five weeks. One brood is normal.

Long-tailed Tit *(Aegithalos caudatus)*

A delightful resident bird often seen in family parties in winter, when it will visit gardens, copses and shrubberies and may keep company with other small birds such as titmice in roving flocks. The family groups break up in spring,as long-tailed tits are not communal birds when nesting. They feed in trees, copses, thickets and hedgerows on insects and small seeds. They may come down to a bird table in severe winters for titbits including suet, cheese, fatty foods or even crumbs. Generally speaking, though, long-tailed tits are not bird table feeders.

The nest is a marvellous ball of lichens, fur, grasses, moss and spiders' webs, packed with feathers inside. It is built about five to eight feet from the ground in a dense bush such as hawthorn, black-thorn, gorse or an evergreen, usually a bush with plenty of foliage cover. They are said to nest sometimes as high as 40 feet by the trunk of a tall tree, but I've never seen a nest so high – not that that is surprising! The nest blends in so well that it is often difficult to see. The ball has an entrance hole in one side near the top, in the manner of a wren's nest. It is a very complex and beautiful creation and can take two weeks to build. A pair nests with us each year and we often see the birds making repeated visits to window corners to gather cobwebs used for nest building. It is said that the female builds the nest but I have watched both birds gathering materials together.

The eggs are laid in April or early May, and usually number about eight but can run as high as twelve – counting them is very hard in a tiny, tightly packed nest. They are white with reddish-brown spots particularly towards the larger end, the degree of spotting being subject to considerable variation. Incubation takes about two weeks, fledging a little over two weeks. They are believed to rear only one brood a year, and later nests are probably the result of earlier tragedy. Our pair nested in a dense evergreen shrub last year, but in unseasonable storms the branches were bent and the nest tipped over. We tied the branches back to set the nest upright again with its contents still undamaged but, despite staying nearby for a day or two, the parents finally deserted. This year they nested in a young spruce tree twenty yards away.

They are charming birds and a pleasure to have in any garden. They seem more common than they were a few years ago, in my area at least. There is little you can do to attract them to your garden beyond providing the right kind of nesting shrubs. They seem to prefer an open aspect as provided by an isolated shrub of their choice rather than one amongst a hedgerow of others. Alternatively, a hedgerow bush left proud above a lower hedge may have the same attraction.

Mistle Thrush *(Turdus viscivorus)*
Sometimes known as the storm cock, supposedly from its habit of singing away regardless of bad weather, which is probably a result of its being an early nester. It is a resident bird but less common than the song thrush and not so likely to visit gardens, and then only the larger ones.

These birds have been known to take food left out for them in hard winter weather but otherwise are very independent. They feed mainly on insects and fruit, including all manner of berries in season, and they are not regular visitors to bird tables.

The nest is like an untidy version of a song thrush's nest, but with a lining of grass. Usually it is placed quite high in an upper fork of a tree, or where a branch joins the stem. They often nest early, some nests being built in February when, with no leaf cover, the nest may be plainly visible. When available, they will often choose a tall holly tree or a conifer such as cypress, in which case the nest may go unseen. The nest will normally be placed higher than fifteen feet and even as high as thirty.

Four or five eggs are the normal clutch, usually laid in March. The ground colour is creamy or greeny white with spots and splashes of red-brown or grey. Incubation and fledging each take about two weeks. Two broods are often reared in a season.

You cannot do much to attract mistle thrushes, other than provide tall trees and perhaps berry-bearing shrubs. If you have none initially, then cypress is your best bet.

Moorhen *(Gallinula chloropus)*

Not found on moors. The name is believed to be a corruption of merehen, a bird of meres, an old name for still water lakes, and they are often popularly known as waterhens. If you have the right kind of pond, and it would need to be over ten feet in diameter, there is a chance you may attract moorhens, which are resident birds and our commonest waterfowl apart from the mallard. Moorhens will come to a small pond or stream quite readily in situations where mallard will not, as mallard usually like a larger expanse of water with an open aspect to give them a clear flight path to escape. A moorhen, on the other hand, will usually escape danger by creeping away or by scurrying and flying only a short distance, using all the available cover in which to hide. They will frequent marshy fields, dykes, and water ditches even in towns and cities, as long as there is plenty of vegetation around. A bare concrete pond is unlikely to ever see a moorhen.

Moorhens are initially shy and cautious birds, particularly when nesting. They spend much time exploring amongst reed beds or on open water or pond edges, and usually will fly only when startled. To attract moorhens you must create the kind of environment they enjoy – namely clusters of reeds, irises, bulrushes or any sort of dense pondside vegetation, where they can hide if they feel threatened and where they can nest. If you have room to build a small island-like clump of tall vegetation (pond irises are ideal) surrounded by water, this helps, though they are happy enough with any pondside herbage. Moorhens also like to bathe in the shallows and share with other water birds a love of "paddling": that is, standing with their feet and legs in shallow water, especially in flowing water. A small submerged 'island' made from a few stones an inch or so below the surface can be very popular.

On my own pond moorhens will often stand, usually singly, in the shallows enjoying the warmth of the sun during the first hour or two of sunlight, especially in winter. Once they get used to your pond, moorhens soon lose their shyness. My own pond is only some twenty yards or so from the house, yet my moorhens will not bother to fly away at the appearance of humans, but will casually stroll into the herbage, where they can keep an eye on you whilst half-hidden themselves. They never become really tame, but do learn to accept passers-by.

For a nesting site, moorhens will use a small, reedy island or promontory, where reeds reach into the water or low bushes hang close to the surface. They cannot nest on your pond unless you provide suitable vegetation.

Moorhens pair up during March or even earlier and will start building during April. Often a bird will be seen picking up a twig and throwing it over its back, which is a sign they are thinking about building.

The nest is a platform woven from strands of reed and grasses, and perhaps twigs, raised a few inches above water level and usually built by the water's edge or on some extended reach of foliage well out over the water. The eggs are sometimes visible from above, though concealed from the side. They are said to keep adding nest material to raise the nest level during floods. In fact, moorhens seem to enjoy adding material regardless of water level. Despite a constant water level, my own nesting birds will go on evening patrol each day looking for choice new grass pieces to add to the nest, even after the young have hatched out. They particularly like the dead grassy stalks of bulrushes for this purpose.

More than one nest is usually built, from which one is ultimately chosen. The clutch will number from six to ten tan-coloured eggs mottled with blotches of red and dark brown. Incubation lasts three weeks and they will raise two, or even three, broods in a season. Young from early broods will stay with the parents and even help to feed the young of later broods that year.

Moorhens seldom move away from their summer haunts and a regular supply of food will ensure they don't. Our own moorhens soon learned to come to the bank to steal chicken pellets, and food put out this way will soon entice them on a regular basis. They eat small insects but much prefer easy pickings in the form of provided food. At one time our moorhens learned that a constant supply of chicken food was available in our chicken hut and we would watch a whole procession of parents and young of three different sizes from three successive broods of that year entering the hut for feed each day.

They like to roost in reeds and may be seen bending down reed stems to reach the water, thereby making a kind of sloping ladder which they can walk up, especially the young ones, for roosting a foot or so above the water. They will do this even though there might be bushes with low branches already overhanging the water.

Moorhens seem to eat anything a domestic chicken will take readily and they soon learn to hold their own at a food trough against chickens or hen pheasants, though not a cock pheasant. They are strongly territorial in the breeding season and once a pair has settled in, it will drive any others away from a small pond. They are more aggressive in the breeding season and rival males may fight quite fiercely with much noise and flying feathers.

Nuthatch *(Sitta europaea)*

A resident bird of open woodland, parks, copses and gardens. Mature trees are its main requirement, where it can search bark crevices for insects and seeds. It seems to favour trees such as alders with plenty of leaf but without dense foliage. It is very fond of peanuts and will readily visit bird tables for its favourite foods. When eating nuts, it taps noisily at them and can be heard some yards away, being second only to the great spotted woodpecker in this noisy talent. A nuthatch's beak is a formidable weapon and most bird table feeders will readily give way to it at feeding time, with the exception of woodpeckers. They will even crack the shells of hard nuts such as hazelnuts to get at the contents. Try wedging one or two into crevices where you can watch the proceedings.

Nuthatches also like fats, suet and marrowbones, and will eat some seeds and occasionally breadcrumbs and cake crumbs. They feed just as happily upside down as right way up.

They will take willingly to enclosed nest boxes with a 1¼-inch entrance hole. I find the best height is about six to eight feet. They usually plaster mud around the entrance to create a personal touch and often will plaster it along joints in the box too, probably for draught proofing. In nature this hole plastering is to reduce an over-size hole to suit their tastes, but they do it even with a 1¼-inch hole, which is already a tight squeeze for them. It is presumably a habit they can't throw, and no other British bird does this. They will some-times peck at a hole to enlarge it before they reduce its size again with mud! They may begin plastering two or three different boxes before finally settling on the one they want to use. I've watched them do this on boxes in my own garden which were some yards apart and it appears to be more a matter of indecision than confusion.

They are colourful and lively birds, darting about busily in a jerky manner as they work their way apparently at random up or down a tree trunk seeking insects. They are the only birds which will climb down a tree trunk head first.

The nest is built of wood chips and bits of bark, sometimes with a few leaves. The eggs usually number between six and nine and are laid at the end of April or early May. They are white with red-brown spots, not unlike eggs of the tit family. Incubation takes about two weeks and fledging roughly the same. One brood is normal. During nesting nuthatches become less evident. By the time the eggs hatch, the female's plumage has usually picked up a dirty and unkempt appearance from being confined. The parents will bring the young to the bird table for peanuts shortly after they can fly, when the whole family party may come down together.

We have one pair which nests annually in enclosed boxes, selecting a different box each year but all within a twenty-yard-long stretch of trees. Only one pair nests with us each season, though they raise several youngsters, so the young must be driven off to nest elsewhere. We have massive, ancient alder trees along one boundary, which is where they nest, and it may well be these that attract the birds to our garden in the first place – and the constant availability of peanuts.

Pheasant *(Phasianus colchicus)*
Unlikely to visit suburban gardens, but will come to larger or more open gardens in rural or semi-rural situations. Many birds are artificially reared today and are accustomed to being fed, which may account for the tameness some birds soon show. But even birds breeding wild will accept a garden as part of their territory, which they tend to patrol regularly, often on a set morning and evening route. One cock may stroll in the company of several hens, and sometimes other young cocks too, until the nesting season approaches, when cocks become aggressively territorial and will chase off other males. The season's brood often stays as a family party through the autumn and winter.

Pheasants soon become quite tame and will learn to come for feed at a regular time, for instance along with domestic poultry. When I put down food pellets for my chickens each morning, there are frequently as many as four or five pheasants waiting and they will stroll tamely about my feet, even venturing to peck from the container in my hand. During the breeding season both cocks and hens are more secretive and far less tame. But at other times, once a cock pheasant is familiar with a food trough, he will keep farmyard hens or ducks at bay till he has eaten his fill.

They will eat most household scraps and titbits as well as corn and poultry food. Pheasants spend most of their days wandering through shrubbery and wood-edge undergrowth, feeding amongst the leaf litter. They enjoy dust-bathing in a favourite dry spot, such as amongst debris under a conifer, especially in late afternoon sunshine. I often watch them doing this from my study window as several pheasants will wait to take turns at dust-bathing in the dry soil under a cypress tree, and sometimes two will share the same bath. When accustomed to people, they will walk quite unconcerned even past strangers.

Those who feed pheasants need not be particularly anxious for them in the shooting season (October 1 to February 1), since birds that become tame are less likely to be shot. Shooters only shoot flying birds. Pheasants are reluctant to fly at the best of times, even when driven from cover by beaters on a shoot. Tame birds are much more likely to walk away or run for cover, so if your tame birds stray to nearby shooting land, there is every chance they will come back safely. Pheasants soon learn wily ways, and if your garden is near a shoot, you'll find a sudden influx of pheasants coming for sanctuary on shoot days.

Pheasants, especially cock birds, often have variations in plumage which can make individual birds easily identifiable, rather like farmyard poultry.

The hen pheasant will make her sparse nest of grass on the ground in any quiet corner amongst tall grasses or undergrowth, often by a wall or bank for shelter, sometimes under a bramble clump, and usually close to a wood edge rather than in the wood itself. Any sheltered corner with cover will do. A sitting bird can be almost invisible, and they often sit very tight. The plain, olive-coloured eggs usually number ten or twelve but can range from eight to fifteen. They are laid from late April onwards, and one brood is normal each season. The eggs take three to $3\frac{1}{2}$ weeks to hatch, the young twelve days to fledge. Young leave the nest soon after hatching, when the hen takes them into grass or other cover. Be cautious of approaching at this stage as the young easily scatter and, because of their camouflage, are in danger of being walked on.

The cock birds seem to take little part in nesting activities and a cock may have more than one hen nesting in different areas of his territory. Once the young hatch, the cock will often accompany the family party, and families may stay together through much of the winter. Because of this, it is noticeable how a family group of perhaps ten birds may be down to half that number before spring, on account of natural casualties.

You cannot construct a nest site for pheasants, only conditions in which they might choose to nest: odd clusters of brambles amongst dense and overgrown grass, perhaps supported by a few twigs to make foliated cover. These artificial cover spots will appeal to pheasants and often to other smaller nesting birds.

Pheasants have the same odd habits as starlings, in that the hen will sometimes lay a solitary egg on a lawn or some quite unexpected place, so if you come across one, don't imagine you have stumbled across a nest in the middle of your lawn.

Pied Flycatcher *(Ficedula hypoleuca)*

Summer residents arriving in their breeding haunts at the end of April or early May. My usual pair arrived this year on May 1 and were inspecting a nest box that very day, which they built in two weeks later. This was a different nest box from the one they used the previous year but was within twenty yards of the old one. This year's box was *in situ* last year, so why they decided on a change I cannot say. Both boxes face south and are about seven feet high.

Pied flycatchers are birds of woodland and copses, especially old, deciduous woods, which are light and open and where they may find a nesting hole. These are more likely homes than younger woods or dense conifer plantations. They like a stream or a stretch of water nearby, perhaps because water usually provides an abundance of insects on which they feed whilst on the wing. Typical feeding behaviour is to hunt for a few seconds, then return to one of several nearby perches, and the birds will do this time and time again. They cannot be attracted to a bird table by putting out food. One frequently comes to my bird table, which it regards purely as a perching post.

They are not common birds everywhere and are really found only where there is old woodland or copses, especially near water, and mainly in hill country in northern England and Wales. They will visit gardens if you have some woodland nearby or a wooded part in your garden, and they will take readily to enclosed nest boxes, like many hole nesters. They return to the same territory each year and often will nest close to their former site, even in the same box as the previous year. In my own garden I have a surplus of boxes and so my birds are probably spoilt for choice. As they arrive after other hole nesters, such as titmice, who have already begun nesting, they have to select from whatever boxes remain available to them. Nesting holes are usually scarce by May, so you may attract them if you have a few surplus boxes still unoccupied by tits at that time.

They will take boxes with entrance hole sizes of 1⅛ to 1½ inches or bigger, but mine are all 1¼ inch, which seems to suit them. A height of between six and ten feet should be about right, though in the wild they are sometimes obliged to find a higher hole. Sometimes they will nest in a hole in a wall, but a tree hole is the usual choice, which is probably why they take so well to nest boxes. The birds like to have a tree branch conveniently close, but not near, to the entrance, and certainly not a perch on the box itself. A distance of about six feet would be ideal, as the birds like to perch for a moment before flitting to the box. If you don't have a convenient tree branch, knock a stake into the ground for a perching post.

The male often arrives back at the breeding territory ahead of the female and he seems to be the principal one who selects the nest hole. I have watched both birds together investigating possible nest boxes before selecting one, which suggests that the male does not (as sometimes stated) choose the site before she arrives. The female does the building, though the male constantly escorts her and draws her to the chosen site by calling and repeatedly entering the hole himself.

Nesting takes place in May, the clutch of pale blue eggs usually numbering between five and seven, but sometimes more. Incubation takes just under two weeks and fledging the same. One brood is normal.

Pied flycatchers spend much time feeding on the wing within the branches of trees rather than out in the open, so they can be over-looked. On the other hand, they are not shy birds and often will continue feeding regardless of human presence. This year my pair continued nest building oblivious to my presence only eight feet away. They are delightful birds and highly distinctive, so you cannot fail to recognise them. The male is black and white and the female a more subdued brown and white. They are restless birds and have the short bursts of erratic flight typical of all flycatchers.

Pied Wagtail *(Motacilla alba yarrellii)*

A delightful bird and the commonest of the wagtails, often frequent-ing gardens as well as farmyards. It is resident all year round. Pied wagtails are fond of water, whether ponds, streams or other wet places. They often haunt places near human habitation, perhaps because the abundance of buildings offers many nest sites, and frequently they will go about their business having little regard to the presence of people.

They feed essentially on insects and spend much time inspecting lawns and grassy areas, working the same territory over and over again and still coming up with more insects. As I write, a pair are feeding on a patch of lawn outside my window, where they come once or twice each day almost to a regular timetable. It is said they will take crumbs and food scraps. I've never found my birds to do that, but as they wander away outside the breeding season I cannot judge their feeding habits in hard winter weather.

The pied wagtail nests in crevices, gaps or ledges in walls, on window sills, gaps under eaves of a low roof, gaps between slates in a roof: in fact, in a wide variety of places where some sort of half-concealed ledge or support offers a suitable place. The height can be anywhere from about four feet to as much as twenty, but usually in the lower reaches. In my own garden, the same pair of birds has twice nested in ivy against a wall, once in a clematis against a wall, once in an urn on a wall recess, all between six and eight feet high; then in a dovecote fourteen feet high, on a roof rafter twenty feet high via a gap in the slates, and in an open-ended drainpipe five feet high. Almost all these nests were within a twenty-square-yard area, though perhaps they were lucky they had so many options available.

Pied wagtails are fickle in their choice of site and sometimes select some very eccentric places. The nest is built of grass, moss and roots, lined with wool and down, and is usually well hidden, especially from above. They will take to open-fronted nest boxes or possibly flat nesting trays if positioned carefully, such as amongst ivy or an overhang of a window sill. A plentiful supply of insect food in lawns and flower beds may bring them to visit, but the availability of suitable nesting sites is the essential ingredient to induce them to stay.

The eggs number from four to six and have a greyish-white ground colour with small specks and spots of dark grey or grey-black. They are laid in late April, taking roughly two weeks to hatch and the young two weeks to fledge. Two broods will be reared in a season, sometimes three. Pied wagtails are regular victims of cuckoos. If a cuckoo lays in a wagtail's nest, its egg is distinctly larger than the wagtail's own and will stand out easily.

They will return to the same site year after year and might decide to renovate a former nest or might just as likely build a new one close by, probably within a few yards, if circumstances permit. They are resident birds, though mine always move elsewhere in the winter, probably for easier pickings.

Robin *(Erithacus rubecula)*

A resident bird and perhaps our best-known garden visitor, which will eat a great variety of household scraps as well as insects, spiders and worms. Robins seem to be particularly keen to watch out for worms uncovered by the digging gardener. Some robins still nest in wild situations not far removed from those of their distant past. A good many others, however, have learned to exploit the ready availability of food near human dwellings, so that today many pairs nest in gardens and parkland. Those birds which visit gardens grow very familiar and will eat almost anything – some even learn to take food from the hand. So if you have something to offer in the way of food or water, robins are likely to visit you.

Those living in country lanes far from human habitation like a blend of trees with undergrowth, offering them maximum feeding possibilities. Here they may nest in a bank, especially a roadside bank, a hole in a dry stone wall or rock face, under a tussock of grass or perhaps in a hollow log or tree cavity. Garden robins soon learn to take advantage of man-made cavities and may nest in a variety of unusual places which substitute for natural sites – an open-fronted nest box, a flowerpot, a discarded tin can, a hanging flower basket or any convenient cranny or hole in a wall or ivy-covered fence. In both locations robins will sometimes nest in the dense lower cover of trees or bushes. In my garden this year we had a nest in an open drainpipe six feet up a wall, in the base of an over-grown shrub two feet from the ground, and on the ground under a grass tussock. So the height may vary from ground level to about six feet, above which is unusual. Most nests seem to be between two feet and four feet high, and I would suggest four feet as a safe height for an open-fronted nest box. Some covering from a wall creeper would be an advantage.

The nest is built of leaves, roots and hairs. The four to six sandy coloured eggs with light red spots in varying degrees of intensity may be laid as early as the end of March but more often in early April. Incubation takes two weeks, fledging about the same. Two broods may be reared, occasionally three.

In winter robins occupy a solitary territory, which is why it is rare to see more than one bird at a bird table at the same time at this season.

Song Thrush *(Turdus philomelos)*

One of our best-known garden birds, visiting gardens at all times of year and often becoming quite tame in the process, though always wary. It is not overfond of eating at bird tables and usually keeps itself at a safe distance. Its diet consists mostly of worms, snails and the like and also berries such as elder, ivy, mountain ash and black-berries, and it prefers its natural diet to food put out for it. Lawns and shrubberies are favourite feeding places, amongst grass and leaf litter. In hard weather, of course, it is a different story.

The thrush nests in hedges, bushes and conifers. Early nests are often in evergreens such as cypress or ivy. The height is usually between about five feet and seven feet from the ground. To encourage them, plant the right evergreens, especially if trimmed to tall hedge height.

The nest is built of grasses lined with raw mud or cow dung to a smooth, hard finish, distinguishing it from the blackbird's otherwise similar nest, where the mud cup has a grass lining. It will sometimes nest on ledges or window sills, shelves in outbuildings, a tread of a stepladder, or on top of a roll of netting, showing the fickleness which many ledge nesters adopt. It occasionally takes to an open-fronted type of nest box, though none has ever taken to mine.

Thrushes are amongst the earliest nesters and may often have eggs by the last week of March, more commonly in early April. The eggs usually number four or five and are pale blue with black and dark brown spots and dots, the spots often clustered more heavily round the wider end. Incubation takes two weeks, fledging about the same. Two or three broods are raised in a season.

Song thrushes are amongst the few birds that will occasionally lay 'erythristic' eggs. This is quite a mouthful but means eggs of a freak colouring, the ground of such eggs being pinkish or close to white. A bird laying such eggs will do so consistently and its progress can be followed from season to season, nest to nest. I've never found such eggs myself, however, despite having looked for over 40 years, though I have come across eggs of the usual blue background with no spots at all, which are not as rare. A bird laying erythristic eggs may itself have normal or abnormal plumage, and may not be identifiable except through its eggs. Spotting on song thrush eggs can vary greatly even within the same clutch. All of this makes examining the contents of a song thrush nest potentially more interesting than those of birds with unvarying eggs, despite the fact that they are common birds.

Starling *(Sturnus vulgaris)*

A resident bird which needs no description as it commonly nests in roof eaves, rain gutters, holes in walls and in trees. Starlings will eat almost anything including worms, insects, seeds and almost any household food scraps we might put out for other birds. They are greedy feeders and, being larger than most bird table feeders, tend to drive other birds off and eat the first pickings, They are, therefore, not much loved by bird gardeners and not many of us go out of our way to cater for them.

On the other hand, they are cheerful, lively birds which eat a great many harmful insects as well, perhaps, as eating your soft fruits. If you live in the heart of a city and lack many of the garden visitors described in this book, then you may well derive many hours of pleasure from watching starlings and their antics. They are great bathers, both in water and dust-baths. They welcome almost any household scraps and can become quite tame. Starlings often mimic other birds or human whistling in their song and are fine entertainers.

Starlings have grown accustomed to nesting near human habitations, where these sites replace the cliff nesting places they would originally have used. They make an untidy nest of straw and feathers in any convenient hole. They will often take to an enclosed nest box with a two-inch entrance hole, a floor size of not less than eight inches by eight inches, and a depth of ten inches. Site the box high up, preferably under the house eaves. The four to six glossy, pale blue eggs are laid in April. Incubation takes roughly two weeks, fledging about three. Two broods may be reared in a season. They are rather messy nesters and a pair will use the same nest site year after year.

Like one or two other common birds, starlings have the odd habit of laying an egg on a lawn or vegetable patch, presumably because the bird is caught unexpectedly away from the nest when laying time is due.

Oddly enough, we seldom see a starling in our garden. This may be on account of the lack of nesting sites, as I have no nest boxes of a size big enough to admit them.

Swallow *(Hirundo rustica)*

Arrives back in Britain in April after wintering in the tropics and is with us till about October. In prehistoric times the swallow would have nested against inland cliffs or caves or rocky overhangs and, in fact, a few still do so today. But nowadays they seek alternatives such as permanently open barns and outbuildings, garages and carports. Unless you have such facilities, you cannot expect swallows to nest in your garden as, unlike house martins, they are not usually attracted to the eaves of houses but prefer a deeper overhang and a darker, more private place.

Swallows spend much of their time on the wing as they sweep across lawns and fields catching insects. They cannot do that in a tiny garden, so if you haven't the space you are unlikely to have them feeding over your garden. However, they do need water and will come down to rest by the shallows of a pond to drink and also to bathe, apart from which they seldom come to rest on the ground. They also need to gather mud for their nest building, and where better than in the soft, muddy shallows of a garden pond? So even if you haven't a wide expanse of garden, the presence of a pond can bring swallows to you. Insects often abound immediately above the surface of a pond and swallows will scoop these up as they pass back and forth, so for a smaller garden a pond may be the only way to attract them. They will certainly not come down for any kind of food you might be able to put out for them.

If you have a larger pond, you may see swallows drinking in flight, when they swoop low over the water surface and scoop up a mouthful of water in passing.

Swallows usually start to nest in May. The nest is built mostly of mud, forming a cup into which grass is woven with feathers for a lining. The height depends on the building being used and therefore will usually be between six and ten feet, but could be much higher. At different times we have had them nest as low as six feet and as high as twenty in our outbuildings. They prefer to nest on a ledge such as a beam or an angled rafter some little way below a roof or ceiling with a gap of six to eighteen inches between beam and roof. In such a preferred site they will rest the nest on top of the beam, or half on it. If no suitable beam is available, they can glue the nest direct to a wall or beam, almost like an open-topped house martin's nest with the entrance up against the roof.

If you have a suitable building where access is permanently open (an opening three feet square is plenty), they may decide to use it. In one of our buildings they used to swoop down at great speed to fly in through an opening of only six inches square. Swallows will often prospect for new sites prior to nesting, flying in and out of barns and garages before deciding on the right spot. You can try to encourage them by fixing some sort of batten to the wall, like a narrow shelf, some twelve inches or so below the ceiling to offer some nest support.

Often three or four pairs may nest in the same building as a small colony, sometimes many more pairs if the site is large enough. The eggs number from four to six, sometimes more, and are of a white ground colour with spots varying from red-brown to near black. Incubation takes two weeks, fledging 2½ to 3. More than one brood is normal, sometimes several broods in a season, and it is by no means unusual for them to be still feeding young in August. For second and third broods of the season, they may decide to build fresh nests. Once they take to a site, they will come back year after year, either restoring an old nest or building a new one nearby, till prevented by disaster en route or a change in site conditions.

Our own swallow population keeps reducing. We used to have four nesting pairs and are now down to only a single pair. This is despite the fact that successful broods have left each nest each year. From a population of at least four pairs and their numerous offspring of several seasons, this year only three birds returned to our garden, presumably due to fatalities in migration.

Swallows often rest on overhead wires or roof peaks, especially when taking in the early morning sun, and when gathering prior to migration. They are beautiful birds which frequently seem to pay little attention to human presence nearby. Swallows carry waste sacs from their young out of the nests and drop them in flight after a dozen yards or more. If that's where you park your car, best move it!

Town pigeon *(Columba livia)*
Common everywhere in built-up areas and descended from the rock dove, which now exists in its pure form only on remote cliffs. The feral pigeon is the name usually given to the town bird, which is very much interbred with escaped racing varieties and carrier pigeons, so that all manner of colour permutations now appear, as well as such varieties as fantails, popular in dovecotes.

This bird has thrived on man's generosity and in many parks and squares will take food from the hand. If your interest is in racing pigeons, then this is a whole world of its own and outside my scope here. The usual way of encouraging doves is by a dovecote, which allows several pairs to nest together, though you may need to start off with a domesticated pair. A friend of mine bought a pair of white fantails and a dovecote and within a very few years dozens of them roosted round the house like white gargoyles and stalactites of guano adorned every doorway. So be warned, they breed prolifically and have few enemies, except the people whose house they roost on.

Feral pigeons make a nest of a few twigs any time from March onwards or even earlier. They lay a clutch of two white eggs, which take 2½ weeks to hatch and four to five weeks to fledge. They will rear several broods in succession until late autumn or even, in some areas, in to the winter.

Tree Creeper *(Certhia familiaris)*
A resident bird found mainly in open woodland and copses, particularly those with mature trees, where it can search bark crevices for insects, which are its main food. It moves with a jerky, stop-start action as it works its way up a tree trunk, often in a spiral manner. It is the only small British bird to have the unusual, long, downward-curving beak, ideal for picking food from cracks in tree bark. It will often continue feeding apparently unconcerned by human presence. Having climbed up a tree, it will then drop back to the base of the same, or a different, tree and work its way up all over again, preferring always to feed in an upward direction.

Nest building begins in May. Usually a cavity in the bark of a tree is selected, or perhaps a gap where ivy joins a tree trunk or a loose

piece of bark stands proud from the rest. The height could be anywhere from three feet to 30, and the same site may be used year after
year. The nest is built of grass and mosses lined with feathers. The
eggs are white with red-brown spots and number from five to seven,
rarely more. They are laid in May or early June. Incubation and
fledging each take about two weeks and one brood is usual.

The tree creeper is a slit nester. Various designs of nest box have
been tried in an attempt to cater for its taste. These have a main
entrance slit rather than a hole, sometimes with a second one as a
kind of emergency exit/rear door. Pieces of bark wired to tree trunks
to form a simulated site may work. Special nest boxes tend to be
tapered like a narrow tent with an opening at each end. I've tried
these, but with no success personally.

We have tree creepers in our garden but I have yet to find my first
nest. They inhabit some ancient alder trees growing in a stream and
wedged between a wall and a high bank, which means that access to
search is more or less impossible.

Tree creepers will not come down for bird table food, being insect
eaters, and nest box attraction seems a very hit-and-miss affair with
this species. Probably your only chance of attracting them is to have
mature deciduous trees, especially ivy-covered ones.

Tree sparrow *(Passer montanus)*
Country version of the house sparrow and a resident bird occurring
mostly in woodland, parkland and gardens, provided they have
mature trees. It is by no means common everywhere. It feeds on
insects and spiders but principally seeds. It will take food from a bird
table but is not nearly as trusting as the house sparrow. I've never
seen tree sparrows at my bird table nor even in my garden, but that
could be due to location.

They nest in holes in trees and sometimes in the base of old nests
of crows or rooks, or even in occupied nests. Pairs will occasionally
nest in close proximity to others of the same species, like a small
colony. They will nest in enclosed boxes with an optimum hole size
1⅛ inch in diameter, but I would use 1¼ inch. Site it on the high
side of ten feet.

The nest is an untidy affair of grass and feathers. The clutch of
four to six eggs is laid in May. They have a dull white ground colour
and are covered in brown and dark-brown splashes with considerable variation, sometimes even in the same clutch. Incubation and
fledging each take roughly two weeks. Two broods are often reared
in a season.

Woodpigeon *(Columba palumbus)*

A resident bird and identifiable by its prominent white neck patch and white wing flash when flying. It is a handsome bird but little loved by farmers or vegetable gardeners as its food includes cereals and also leaf vegetables. It is very widespread and will visit gardens in towns as well as in the countryside.

Woodpigeons will come to bird tables to feed, or more readily to the ground, and will eat seeds, selected household scraps and peas and beans as well as bread.

The nest is very thinly built platform of twigs seldom less than eight feet high and often much higher. It is so thinly built that often you can see whether it contains eggs or young simply by looking up from the ground. The nest is often on a lateral branch of a tall shrub or evergreen such as a cypress or hawthorn bush, or indeed anywhere as long as some leaf cover will surround it. Level branches of large, ivy-covered trees are popular sites. They may nest as early as March but the first eggs are more usual in April. The eggs are pure white and only two are laid per clutch. Incubation takes 2½ weeks, fledging three weeks or a little more. Two broods or even more will be reared in a season.

These birds make little attempt at secrecy and if they are nesting in your garden, you'll be in no doubt about it. A few years ago we had a single pair nesting in our garden and their gentle cooing was a soothing and restful sound. This year we have six pairs and vegetable-growing neighbours are getting restless. Magpies account for a good number of woodpigeon eggs, probably because the nests are not usually hard to spot.

Wren *(Troglodytes troglodytes)*

A charming bird known to everyone. It seems to be ever on the move, searching crevices and cracks in walls and undergrowth. It nests in crevices, holes, cracks is masonry, ledges and the like, sometimes in the old nests of other birds. To encourage it to visit and nest, you need to create the kind of environment it enjoys, and clearly a plain and bare rectangular garden plot is not adequate. If you have any old buildings in your garden such as stables, lean-to's or tumbledown sheds, it will often find an unused corner or ledge to build on. Just occasionally it will use a tit box or an open-fronted nest box of the type made for robins. A pair twice nested in an old swallow's nest on a rafter in our barn; another pair on a beam in a coal shed with a permanently open door; another in thick ivy on a tree trunk. Old wood piles or bundles of sticks tied in a garden corner may encourage them, especially if partly overgrown with grasses so the nest might pass unnoticed amongst other leaf litter. Ivy-covered walls can tempt them, especially if old dry stone walls or ones with crumbling mortar. Ivy-covered or overgrown banks, an old kettle or paint can wedged in a mossy wall corner, these are the kind of tucked-away places they prefer.

The nest is a ball of leaves and grasses with an entrance hole in the side. It is seldom more than five or six feet from the ground, though different pairs of wrens in my own garden regularly nest higher – at about the seven- or eight-foot level. The eggs number anywhere from five to eight and are laid any time from late April. Several nests are usually built, of which one is finally chosen for the eggs.

Wrens are not particularly bird table feeders, though they will sometimes hunt for crumbs that have fallen to the ground below one. They are more likely to search for insects and spiders in overgrown, quiet corners and undergrowth. The eggs hatch in about two weeks, and in just more than another two weeks the young will leave the nest.

On the whole wrens like uncared-for and "scruffy", neglected corners, which might be inconsistent with your idea of a trim garden. If you want to encourage them in a tidy garden, your only chance is to go for the odd unused corners where bits of lumber offer nooks and crannies.